Also by Jeffrey Moussaieff Masson

The Pig Who Sang to the Moon: The Emotional World of Farm Animals

The Nine Emotional Lives of Cats: A Journey into the Feline Heart

The Evolution of Fatherhood: A Celebration of Animal and Human Families

Dogs Never Lie About Love: Reflections on the Emotional World of Dogs

The Wild Child: The Unsolved Mystery of Kaspar Hauser

When Elephants Weep: The Emotional Lives of Animals
  (with Susan McCarthy)

My Father's Guru: A Journey Through Spirituality and Disillusion

Final Analysis: The Making and Unmaking of a Psychoanalyst

Against Therapy: Emotional Tyranny and the Myth of Psychological Healing

A Dark Science: Women, Sexuality, and Psychiatry in the Nineteenth Century

The Assault on Truth: Freud's Suppression of the Seduction Theory

The Oceanic Feeling: The Origins of Religious Sentiment in Ancient India

The Complete Letters of Sigmund Freud to Wilhelm Fliess 1887–1904 (editor)

The Peacock's Egg: Love Poems from Ancient India
  (editor, translations by W. S. Merwin)

The Dhvanyaloka of Anandavardhana with the Locana of Abhinavagupta
  (translator, with D. H. H. Ingalls and M. V. Patwardhan)

Love's Enchanted World: The Avimaraka (with D. D. Kosambi)

The Rasadhyaya of the Natyasastra
  (translator and editor, with M. V. Patwardhan; two volumes)

Santarasa and Abhinvagupta's Philosophy of Aesthetics

Dogs Have the Strangest Friends, and Other True Stories of Animal Feelings
  (for children)

Slipping into Paradise

Ballantine Books New York

Slipping into

Paradise

Why I Live in New Zealand

JEFFREY MOUSSAIEFF MASSON

A Ballantine Book
Published by The Random House Publishing Group

Copyright © 2004 by Jeffrey Moussaieff Masson

www.ballantinebooks.com

Library of Congress Cataloging-in-Publication Data

Masson, J. Moussaieff (Jeffrey Moussaieff), 1941–
    Slipping into paradise : why I live in New Zealand / Jeffrey
Moussaieff Masson.— 1st ed.
        p.   cm
    Includes bibliographical references.
    ISBN 0-345-46614-4 (HC)—ISBN 0-345-46634-9 (TR)
        1. New Zealand—Description and travel.   2. New
Zealand—Social life and customs.   3. Masson, J. Moussaieff
(Jeffrey Moussaieff), 1941–   I. Title.

DU413.M37 2004
993.0.—dc22
                                            2004047072
Manufactured in the United States of America

First Edition: August 2004

1   2   3   4   5   6   7   8   9

Book Design by Mercedes Everett

For the light of my life, Leila, and our children,
Ilan and Manu, and my wonderful daughter Simone

Contents

Acknowledgments   xi

Preface: Karaka Bay   xv

1. Why I Live in New Zealand   3

2. The Joy of Living Here as Opposed to There: Comparing Cultures   24

3. Australia Versus New Zealand   42

4. Fifty Important Dates in New Zealand History: A Personal Perspective   53

5. Mad About the Trees, Not to Mention the Birds   88

6. The Trouble with Paradise   139

7. A Conversation with a Great Ordinary Kiwi: Sir Edmund Hillary   155

8. Maori: The People, The Culture, The Language   176

9. A Very Personal Itinerary   193

Conclusion: Should You Move to New Zealand?   222

Recommended Reading   229

Glossary of New Zealand English Words and Expressions   233

Glossary of Maori Words   241

Acknowledgments

Thanks to all the wonderful people of New Zealand, far too numerous to name: neighbors on our beach, strangers, academics, intellectuals, artists, writers, photographers, panel beaters, builders, and expats who spoke to me and encouraged me to write about their unique and beautiful country.

Brent Lewis, who owns the fascinating Nostromo Books, read the entire manuscript and made many useful suggestions. Merimeri Penfold, a commissioner with the Human Rights Commission (Te Kahui Tika Tangata), and a native speaker of Maori, read my Maori glossary and made valuable suggestions. Margaret Orbell, the distinguished classical Maori scholar, read my chapter on the Maori and was most helpful. I want to thank Georgina Bayer, MP, for her interview with me. I am especially grateful to the foreign minister, Phil Goff, who came down to our house and gave me a long and informal interview confirming my benign prejudices about the unique friendliness of New Zealanders, even of those in high places. The same is true of the greatest living icon in New Zealand, Sir Edmund Hillary. My thanks also go to Witi Ihimaera, author of *Whale Rider*. The residents of Karaka Bay, where we live, have been wonderful, supportive neighbors, and are only a bit wary at the unwanted attention this book may bring to them.

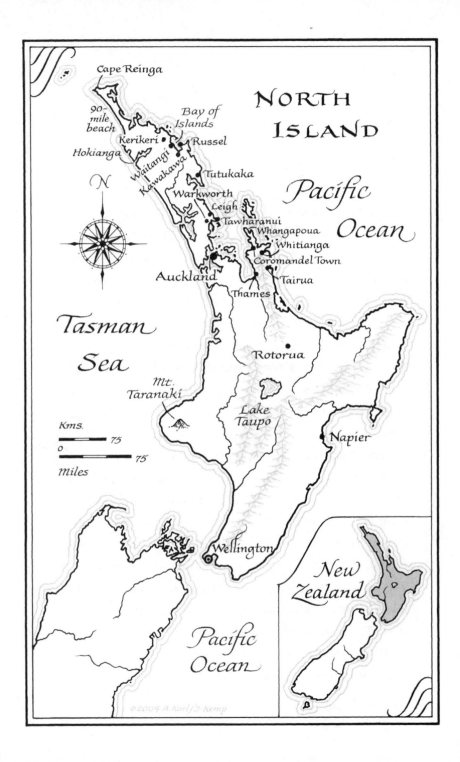

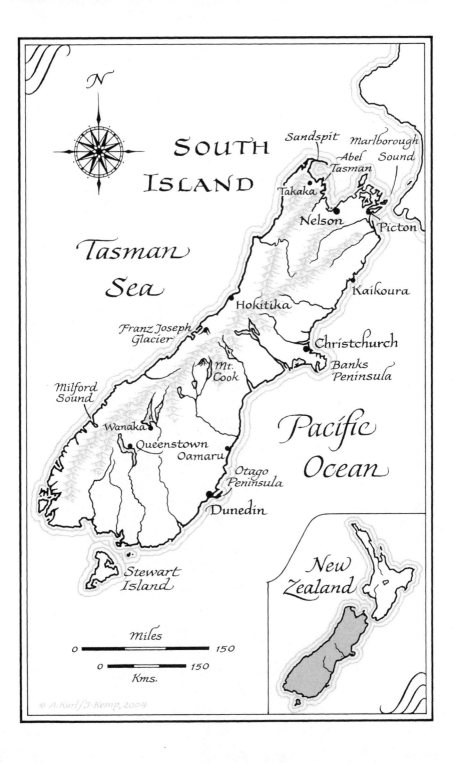

Preface: Karaka Bay

Part memoir, part philosophical reflection, part travel book, this is an account of why I choose to live in New Zealand. Most people do not get to choose where they live; for the vast majority of humans over the past thousands of years, we are born, grow up, live, and die in the same place. In statistical fact, only 3 percent of the world's population lives outside their home country for a year or more. But increasingly, people have become free to decide where they want to live. For most people, especially in America, this means choosing a place within the United States. But more and more people are electing to live somewhere else.

While visiting Australia and New Zealand several years ago, I suddenly realized that I was not forced to live in North America or in Europe. When I stepped off the plane and saw the bright green—the giant fern trees that grow only in New Zealand—and drove through a prehistoric lush forest, arriving at a beach just fifteen minutes from downtown Auckland, and when I realized that there are 365 beaches just one hour's drive from Auckland, I thought: *I have come home.* I had found the perfect spot.

New Zealand is the green gem in the middle of the South Pacific, with southerly airstreams that remove pollution; a place where even the rainfall is clean and refreshing. Moreover, it is a social democracy where women occupy important political posts. The prime minister, Helen Clark, is a woman. The governor general, Dame Silvia Cartwright, is a woman. The attorney general, Margaret Wilson, is a woman. The chief commissioner of the Human Rights Commission is a woman, Rosslyn Noonan.

Egalitarianism is the ruling philosophy; and indeed my wife, a doctor, earns little more than the man building our house. When I walk into the bank, there are toys in a small enclosed area where our eighteen-month-old son, Manu, can play. *Child-friendly* is the term that constantly comes to mind while traveling around New Zealand: Stores have sandboxes, and even the smallest town has an expansive outdoor playground. There are barely four million people in the whole country—three million in the North Island and only one million in the South Island—so when you drive through spectacular scenery, from glacial in the south to subtropical on parts of the North Island where Auckland is located, yours is often the only car on the road. Everybody you meet is curious about you and where you come from, but in a most friendly and unthreatening way. Sound like paradise? Well, in many ways it is. It reminds me of the Hawaii and California I knew as a child, where neighbors talked to one another and there was a definite sense of community, something rapidly disappearing in many places. I think I will never leave!

I wonder if I am the only person to have the feeling that life here is somehow unreal. Auckland, indeed New Zealand itself, feels unreal: so green, so pure, so clean, so friendly, almost like a movie set. It reminds me of the 1998 film *Pleasantville,* even more of *The Truman Show* by Peter Weir with Jim Carrey. You almost expect the director to suddenly announce "Cut!" and all the pleasant people to drop their act and behave in the same rude way the rest of the world has become accustomed to. The palm trees get carted off, the colors fade, the water is sucked back up, the bird-sounds recording is turned off; in short, your paradise is revealed to be nothing but a fraud. Indeed, it is as if you were being set up to believe that this kind of place existed, when in fact it does not. This is partly true. Would the true New Zealand please stand up? Is there such a thing?

New Zealand is a long, thin country on a wide continental shelf. It is 103,737 square miles, roughly the size of Oregon, and with just about the same population. (I have often thought of New Zealand as being a bit like the coastal towns in Oregon; the main difference is that you can swim in these oceans, whereas the only thing you can do in the cold Oregon ocean is surf, if you are suicidal, that is.) The northern part of the North Island, where I live, is a long, narrow peninsula; at no point are you more than eighteen miles from the coast. It has a temperate climate, influenced by the fact that it lies isolated in the middle of two oceans, the Tasman Sea and the southern Pacific Ocean. The North Island is almost seventy thousand square miles. Tectonic collision has molded a young land, which still experiences ruptures and eruptions. The country as a whole is geologically youthful and completely isolated. *Isolation* is a key word to understanding the landscape, the animals, and even, I would claim, the people.

Although officially the climate is temperate, in parts of the North Island it would be more accurate to say the climate is subtropical. Sunshine explains much of the reason we moved here. I have become addicted to sunshine. When I was living in Toronto, and also in London, I became acutely aware of how rarely the sun shines in such places. Louis MacNeice once wrote about how sunlight on the English garden hardens and grows cold and how you cannot "cage the minute within its nets of gold." Here that does not happen. The sunlight lingers. In the evening, as I watch Motukorea, the green volcanic island in front of my house, the fading sunlight illuminates it in a thousand startling ways and the light show seems to continue for hours. Half the island is lit up, then the hillside, then the top, and often the sea around it. It lasts so long I am never certain it has actually ended. There is a bounty of sunlight here that makes you bless your good fortune and feel unconstricted. Perhaps it is simply that you know the next day can possibly bring you rain and sunshine, cold and warmth, winds and calm—all in the same day. The weather is never static here, rarely predictable, and never boring. One reason for this is that New Zealand enjoys a maritime climate, as opposed to a continental climate typical of larger landmasses, meaning we will have sudden, severe changes in weather. It makes itself felt, it impinges upon you in a way that makes you want to yield happily. In Toronto, in London, in Boston, I got the opposite feeling: that states of weather were going to descend not just upon the land, but also upon my spirit, lasting forever, indifferently crushing me and the earth.

When my twenty-nine-year-old daughter, Simone, was visiting Auckland after we first moved here, I took her to some of my favorite places: the volcanic top of Mount Eden, Maraitai, Long Bay, and other beaches, bays, mangrove forests, and the rain forest in Titirangi. At one point I said to her, as a kind of rhetorical device: "I don't know why I love this place so much." Her response took me aback: "Neither do I." She was not being cynical or unpleasant, just asking for more information. Why *did* I love this place so much? People in New Zealand, a recent poll shows, consider themselves extremely lucky to live here. Eighty-five percent would not want to live anywhere else in the world. Always busy thinking alternate possibilities, the other day I began a conversation with my wife, Leila, "If we could live anywhere in the world, where—" but she interrupted me: "Darling, we *can* live anywhere in the world. That is why we are living here."

New Zealanders *and* foreigners do go on and on about the physical beauty of New Zealand. It's not so easy to talk about the beauty of a landscape because we are really talking about a great deal more than landscape. We are talking about *us in* the landscape. While we bring ourselves—and all our baggage— to a place, we really have little effect on that place, whereas the place has a deep effect on us. I don't mean that we can't ruin a landscape—we are amazingly adept at that—I just mean that our own bad mood does not affect the flowers and trees around us. We can contaminate a place physically, but not spiritually, whereas landscapes rarely affect us physically but do so by touching our spirit.

In almost all other countries, we do not often get to see such beautiful places with so few people in them. Now, I have always found it a bit odd that each one of us wants to be the only one to enjoy something; why should we be surprised that if we find something beautiful, someone else does, too, and has as much right to be there as we do? When we visited places he loved, if there were too many people there, my father would always stand apart. He was upset that *his* place was being desecrated. But any other tourist could have, with equal justification, stood back and been angry at *his* presence. Why should he and only he have the privilege of seeing such beauty? Philosophically, I thought my father was foolish. Nonetheless, I could not help feeling the same disappointment myself.

In New Zealand, you don't have to worry about that. The line among locals is that if you go to a beach and you find *one* other family there, you immediately leave to find one less crowded! I can no longer count the number of times we were the only people on the beach, indeed, the only person in a store, on the road, in a restaurant, at a café, at a bus stop, at a rest stop on the road. We have taken walks that are prominently signposted, a two-hour tramp through a lovely kauri forest, and not met a single other person the entire time. Where else can that happen? When you have a country the size of Oregon with only four million people in it, that is what you get. Sometimes it makes you feel lonely; at other times you exult. Of course not everyone revels in the physical beauty of this country. One of the most distinguished persons ever to have lived in New Zealand is Sir Karl Popper, the philosopher and author of the immensely influential *The Open Society and Its Enemies*. But in his autobiography, he has nothing whatsoever to say of the beauty of the country. It seems to have been wasted on him. Not everybody need react as I do.

There is a sense here that the landscape exists without reference to humans, probably because almost more than any other place, humans have been here for only a very short time, less than eight hundred years. (The historian Michael King argues that there is no direct evidence of human occupation of New Zealand before the thirteenth century CE.) Europeans Joseph Banks and James Cook were in New Zealand only in the eighteenth century. By contrast, the European countryside has long been, as Simon Schama puts it, "ribboned with trails, like Ariadne's thread, that are guaranteed to deliver the walker from savagery and get him back to the station in time for the next train to Paris." The New Zealand landscape has nothing savage about it, yet it is singularly devoid of human markers. Thus what Proust once observed about Europe—"The memory of a particular image is but regret for a particular moment; and houses, roads, avenues are as fugitive, alas, as the years"—while beautifully expressed, is of only minimal relevance for New Zealand, where avenues and other emblems of Parisian life are absent. In a sense, the New Zealand landscape dwarfs even memory.

*T*oday is one of those glorious days where the view before me seems almost too beautiful to be real. From where I sit at my desk, with the black-backed gulls wheeling about in perfect arcs, and the strange, almost prehistoric-looking gray herons moving their long legs very deliberately among the rocks and shells at the ocean's edge, I am looking out at Motukorea, a small but perfectly shaped volcanic island. It is just a twenty-minute kayak ride from my beach, and then you climb the green hillside for half an hour to the crater's edge and peer down. Behind it is Waiheke Island, a popular place half an hour's ferry ride from downtown Auckland that has become even more popular in the last year: Real estate prices jumped nearly 100 percent in one year! To the left is Rangitoto, a volcanic island only six hundred years old. Veering off to the right, with a little causeway between them, is Motutapu, which is also a volcanic island, only this one is many millions of years old. Orcas often pass by my house on their way up the estuary—it does not go far, maybe another mile, so I can watch them return.

My beach is less than a quarter mile long, then it turns into rocks on both sides, but at low tide, like right now, I can walk along the volcanic rocks to my little town, St. Heliers, in less than half an hour. Every evening I walk at sunset along the beach, looking for unusual stones (I like the ones with small wormholes in them) and hoping, in vain, to find the rainbow-hued paua ("abalone") shell. There are miniature versions of this exquisite shell, with tiny airholes on the rough outer side. When you turn over the empty shell, you are greeted with a dazzling array of iridescent colors. My son Ilan thinks they will one day be more valuable than money (his logic is irrefutable) and collects them avidly. If I turn right, I come to a neighborhood boat club, and homes along the cliff. The cats like it when I take that route, and follow me for at least a mile along the rocks until we come to a second beach, with an old abandoned boat shed. I have never encountered another person on this walk; maybe that's why the cats wait for it, and seem delighted when they realize that our family is taking "their" walk.

There are tiny clouds now, a very bright sun; it is springtime here, and you can feel it. The weather is mild: seventy degrees, but much hotter in the sun, where I have been sitting most of the day, reading on our deck overlooking the sea, which is at least ten different colors of blue today—but I quickly come to the end of my color vocabulary, from turquoise to sapphire blue (which my father, being a gem merchant, particularly loved) to a tide-pool blue, and the shiny peacock blue, and finally to the deep meridian blue characteristic of these waters of the Hauraki Gulf in front of me. The endless Pacific Ocean, which goes uninterrupted all the way past Hawaii to the coast of Chile, another Pacific Rim country, is just beyond, not visible from where I sit, though the high mountains of the Coromandel Peninsula are, especially on a clear day like today, giving a sense of great distance, of never-ending sea and green mountains that thrills me every time I see it. The grass on the hillside of Motukorea is so green it practically blinds me. I put on sunglasses, but that is worse because they are polarized and simply enhance the colors. (Do they just enhance their recognition? Or do they reveal their true nature—who can say? It is very difficult to argue truth and color.) Leila's play-center group of ten women with their toddlers came to the beach today, and the one woman who was newly arrived from England stood with her mouth agape: "You are in paradise. How can anything but that cliché be used at this moment?" We had to agree. Here is a picture of what I am looking at right now:

Slipping into Paradise

Why I Live in New Zealand

The affair began on the flight from Sydney to Auckland. I was sitting next to a tall, blond woman. She was beautiful. She was young—thirty-four. She was also smart (she had studied at Harvard, the University of California—San Francisco, France, Germany) and spoke five languages fluently. She was a doctor and she had a charming sense of humor. As the plane circled Auckland and I looked out, I realized I was falling in love. Not with her. I already fell in love with her six years previously. She was my wife. I mean with Newzillin (New Zealand). As we circled over Auckland, I could see the whole city laid out beneath me, but what really got my attention were the ocean, the harbor, and the bays. Everywhere you looked there was water, and small green islands with volcanoes on them. It reminded me of Hawaii, and I have always had a soft spot for Hawaii, ever since I lived there as a fourteen-year-old for one year, and then had strange ecstatic dreams about tropical oceans for years after.

When I got off the plane, I saw green hills surrounding the airport. But they were not the green I was used to. This green was like no other green I had ever seen. It was *green* green. And the blue of the water near the airport was *blue* blue. There was a strong breeze blowing in the balmy summer (it was December—remember, reversed seasons in the Southern Hemisphere), as it often blows in Auckland, taking away the little pollution there is. So the light is not distorted in the way it is in Los Angeles. I had just been running in California, at Laguna Beach, where my mother lived, and while I loved the place as you can only love the places of your childhood, I could barely see the hills just a mile or less away, so bad was the smog. Yellow air everywhere. So this is what the world looked like when you were seeing it without interference.

There is a joke about New Zealanders. As soon as you arrive in the customs area at the airport, the officer, sensitive as all New Zealanders are to perceptions of their country, asks: "How do you like New Zealand?" (The mandatory answer of course is: "The most beautiful country on earth," or, as they say here, Godzone.) How on earth, foreigners wonder, can you know when you have just disembarked? But I knew, *I knew.* And it was no joke, the woman at the desk *did* ask me, and I answered truthfully: I am in love! (I am not alone. When my eighty-four-year-old mother had been here for less than a day, she, too, was asked how she liked her new adopted country. Like a nice Jewish lady she always answers a question with a question, so she said, truthfully, "What's not to like?")

People were unbelievably friendly at the airport; there is free coffee and tea, and special lanes at immigration for families with kids. There was a telephone with a big sign: FREE LOCAL CALLS. Volunteers brought carts to arriving passengers, and offered help. There was a small stream with tropical flowers in the middle of the terminal.

We rented a car and started to drive into the city. The breeze was light, the air was warm, and it felt just like the tropics. Everybody was in shorts and sandals. Actually, lots of kids were barefoot—something else I had not seen since I was in the ninth grade in Kailua. We left the airport and were immediately driving alongside a mangrove swamp. Mangroves! Like Bali. Where was I? Was this really a temperate climate? (For the longest time I was convinced the climate here was tropical, or at least semitropical. I was chagrined to learn it was more soberly called temperate.) Sea wherever you looked. And volcanic mountains. *What a paradise,* I thought, feeling like I had been given a drug. I was high on the beauty of this place just driving from the airport. What would happen to me in the next few weeks? Leila worried. She was right. Within two days I told her: "I have found my home." Why did I feel like this? Does it happen to others?

When I was living in Toronto, one cold winter morning I told my analyst (I was in training to become a Freudian analyst—bad mistake) that I missed Los Angeles. "Of course," he said, "it is home." Well, that made sense, it *was* home, for I lived there for most of my childhood. But Auckland, New Zealand? I had never before set foot in this place; how could I feel I had come home? It remains a mystery to me even now, but I find I'll still suddenly feel ecstatic for no good reason just driving along the shore that leads from our house into the center of Auckland. Islands do this to me. Something about being on an island affects me deeply. It is green surrounded by blue. Personally, I think it is deeply rooted in everyone. I am no great fan of sociobiologists (now called evolutionary psychologists), but they have one point I am in agreement with: We have innate, genetically mandated preferences for certain kinds of scenery that involve water and trees. It's really nothing but common sense. If humans evolved in certain climates and landscapes, then to find them again could represent survival, as well as happiness, so it is little surprising that when we see them again, it is if we "recognize" something we already knew. Even hospital patients do better when they look out on green as opposed to a blank wall. *Duh,* as my daughter Simone frequently used to tell me when she was a teenager.

Over the next few days, my seemingly drugged state did not abate. On the contrary, the more I saw, the more certain I was that this was to be my home. I would drive Leila and our three-year-old son Ilan around Auckland, just exploring at random, and I would bang on the steering wheel in wild enthusiasm: "Look at those giant banyan trees!" Wrong: They are Morton Bay fig trees, from Australia, not native at all. "Look at those giant ferns! This could be a million years ago!" (Actually, I got this right: These were pongas, (*Cyathea dealbata*), which grow up to forty-five feet high, New Zealand's tallest tree fern. The uncurled parts of the new shoots look like little babies asleep, and they are edible, a tall native fern. They were indeed here when dinosaurs roamed New Zealand.) There were ferns everywhere. Almost all of the ten thousand known species of ferns grow in New Zealand. "Look, avocado trees! Papaya trees! Guava trees! Banana plants, with stalks of red flowers and yellow bananas hanging down!" I drove aimlessly, in a state of enchantment.

We drove out of downtown, along the water's edge, heading east, following the coast. On my left was the water, filled with what seemed a million sailboats (not far off the correct figure—there is practically one boat for everyone in the country). Hundreds of people jogged along the waterfront (jogging was actually invented in New Zealand), and they cheerfully waved at us. We went past a little beach town, Mission Bay—where everyone seemed to be sitting at a café looking out over the beach—past the next little bay, Kohimarama, and then into St. Heliers, another seaside town. Well, *town* was too big a word for a single street with a bank, a bookstore, a fruit store, a travel shop, a real estate agent, and a post office. Like a scene from a 1950s small American town, women walked along wheeling babies in jogging strollers, or they sat outside the restaurant on the corner, looking out at the magnificent cone of the six-hundred-year-old Rangitoto, the island just two miles offshore that is found in every picture of Auckland. In fact, Auckland is built on volcanoes, and many of them are still, in principle, active.

I kept driving, following the coast. I came to a road, Peacock Street, that was aimed at the sea and said NO EXIT. We parked at the bottom of the road and saw a small path leading down to the ocean. We started walking and found ourselves in a forest of giant pohutukawa trees. They were, I soon learned, possibly a thousand years old, and they were then in bloom with bright red flowers. We passed a tiny monument with a plaque, and stopped to read it. It said something about an 1840 treaty having been signed in this bay, which was called Karaka Bay. I had been browsing through our Rough Guide, and I suddenly realized that the plaque was referring to the signing of the Treaty of Waitangi, the founding document that established New Zealand as a country, a treaty between the indigenous Maori and the recently arrived Europeans. It was the equivalent of the U.S. Declaration of Independence. How could that be? The monument was small, just a rusting tiny spire with names engraved of sixteen local chieftains who had signed the treaty on this spot. In America armed guards would staff this sacred site. Here it looked abandoned.

We walked on. All at once the view opened up and we stared at a vast expanse of ocean with many little green islands just a mile or so offshore. There was a sandy beach with rocks and shells, and a strip of healthy grass along the path. On the other side of the path were ten small houses; such a home is called a *bach* in New Zealand (from "suitable for a bachelor"?). The movie set was in full flower: A few families were picnicking on the beach, children splashed in the shallow water, and a bright yellow kayak was in the ocean, too. "Leila," I said, "this is it."

"Well, actually," she replied, "if we could live here, on this beach, I would move to New Zealand."

*T*his is where we now live, on the beach in Karaka Bay. As I recount it now, it still feels like a dream. And it is true: Had we not driven through Auckland, had we not wandered down the hidden path to the beach, had I not left my card with the neighbors, had I not agreed to buy the house over the phone, et cetera, I could very easily imagine the dream fading. Instead, here we are, in real time: Leila and I and our two children, living, breathing in New Zealand. About to become New Zealanders. Strange. Beyond strange. It could so easily have been otherwise!

Did this really happen? Of course. But how and why? Why do people move their whole family to a completely new place? Sometimes they must. They are sent or they seek an opportunity, a teaching position, some are even banished from their own country. But on a whim? Because they have a fantasy? How many people have ever sat down in a vast travel library and said: "Right, let's *choose* the perfect country"? I had not done that. I had stumbled on New Zealand, though I remember when I told somebody in London that I was going there she said, "Ah, the world's best-kept secret." Yet I was totally unprepared for the magnitude of the *coup de foudre*. It *was* like falling in love, when something in the other person appeals to something you cannot name or define or even know exists. Some kind of affinity obviously links people.

I had a similar experience with Leila. She had come to visit a fellow German, an artist who was living with me in Half Moon

Bay, south of San Francisco. The three of us went for a walk on a deserted beach just down the highway from the house where we lived. I listened to Leila for a few moments, then I said to her: "Look, the Arabs have a word for it, it's called *beshert*, 'it is written.' We are destined for each other." She had such an open look. I liked that she was training to be a pediatrician. I liked her manner, the way she laughed *with*, not *at*. Only half an hour into our walk and I felt smitten. I continued: "We both speak lots of languages—we have lived in lots of countries. We are both, miraculously, vegetarians, and for similar reasons. We are both passionately interested in the Holocaust. We could travel the world together, live a year in each country for the next twenty years. I know I am twenty-five years older than you, but I know this was meant to be. I think we are going to get married."

Leila laughed in a good-natured way. "Yeah, right. One problem, though."

"Oh? And what might that be?"

"I wouldn't even have lunch with you, let alone marry you. *Older* is a euphemism. You are *ancient*. I don't even know anybody as old as you."

I was crushed. Served me right for making such a foolish proposal. Besides, she had a point. Leila was twenty-eight. I was fifty-three. She wanted children and I already had an adult daughter.

But I am getting carried away. I could go on for the next twenty pages telling you how I eventually succeeded in winning Leila over to my side. That is another story. This is about

New Zealand. I just wanted to make the point that, yes, I am impulsive, and yes, I act on fantasies, but also that I have, sometimes, a deep intuition when something is right. I was sure about Leila, and I was sure about New Zealand. Something in me responded to the scent of paradise.

I wasn't wrong about Leila. I got it exactly right, and we have been together now for almost ten years. I have found my soul mate, my best friend, the woman in whose arms I will one day die. I know that. Perhaps there is, though, a fantasy element in my love for New Zealand. After all, my life has been dominated by the search for utopias. I have driven across the United States many times, each time taking a different route. And each time there is a hopeless longing, a fantasy really. It overcomes me at certain moments, usually in the early evening. The sun is about to set. My companion and I have stopped talking, lost in our thoughts. There is a sense of autumn, of leaves turning, of days becoming shorter, of the arrival, soon, of winter. As we drive along there is a signpost for a small town I have never heard of, somewhere in Utah, or Arizona, Montana, Colorado, Northern California, upstate Oregon, or near Seattle. We climb a hill, and then, just before the little town is visible—*wham,* I am hit with my fantasy.

In a few seconds I imagine I will look down into a rich and green valley and will see, nestled in a forest clearing, the town itself. The sun will be setting, and I will suddenly realize that I have come to the town of my dreams. I have dreamed of this particular place. We will drive down the hill and reach the first suburbs. The streets will be wide and trees line them on both sides. The homes are modest, but hardly ordinary. Each one has a large garden in front and in back, but there are no fences, so all the houses seem to share a single enormous yard, filled with trees. And the trees themselves, when not filled with fruit, are filled with children, climbing, in tree houses, on swings. There are hundreds and hundreds of them, and they seem to belong to everyone and no one, as if they were a species apart. They are shouting with pleasure and the excitement of the games they are playing. It is like a giant summer camp, but the play is not organized. It is focused on the trees, which seem almost to participate in the games, to take their pleasure, too. There are ponds everywhere—in some, more children are swimming; in some there are ducks and geese. We will drive through this enchanted town slowly, enjoying every moment. We come to stores and they are all small and personal—an organic vegetable shop, a bookshop, and a shop selling odd-looking rocks. There are no chain stores here. Every block has a couple of vegetarian restaurants, all with tables on the sidewalks. Cars are not permitted in the center of the town, ever, and so grass grows and people are walking about in family groups. It feels as if we have stumbled into a movie set. We have. This town exists only in my imagination.

But New Zealand seemed to me enough like my fantasy that every time some element fit, I would have an "aha" experience. I have been reluctant to give it up, although I find myself needing to modify the idealization on a daily basis. After all, there are few vegetarian restaurants here and not a single pedestrian zone in Auckland, though there ought to be. Cars are permitted everywhere, and there are just a few good book-stores. There are no open markets, like there are in Berkeley and all through Europe. No night markets, like in Thailand. No wonderful outdoor stalls. No fresh sugarcane juice, as there is in the chaotic lively streets of Bombay; no pedestrian zones as in Boulder; there are not bicycles everywhere, as in Holland; not the raucous shouting of a neighborhood in Napoli; no children racing around at midnight, as in the piazzas of Palermo. There isn't the color, the excitement, or the exoticism of India, Sri Lanka, Thailand, Italy, or Vietnam.

Still, much of what I experienced that first day I came off the plane and began exploring Auckland turned out to be by and large true. For one thing, I was struck by how benign, gentle, friendly, and safe everything seemed. Lie down anywhere in the New Zealand countryside and you could sleep all afternoon and wake up as if you were sleeping in a hotel room. There are no snakes. (Mind you, I like snakes. When I was six, I hand-printed a card: JEFFREY MASSON, SNAKE EXPERT.) There are no poisonous frogs, centipedes, tarantulas, or scorpions. There is one poisonous spider, the katipo (related to our black widow), but so shy that I have never met anyone who has even seen one. That is why children walk to school barefoot. Nothing will sting them, bite them, or give them a rash. Swimming here is anxiety-free: There is nothing in the water to hurt, or in the air, or in the rivers, or the lakes, or the gardens that can harm you.

The downside of this is that there are no native mammals. Well, that is not quite true. There is a bat, or, to be exact, there are four native bats: One called the little red flying fox (*Pteropus scapulatus*, if you really want to know) has never established itself anywhere (so probably nobody today has ever seen one), and of the remaining three, one, the greater New Zealand short-tailed bat, is extinct, and the other two, a long-tailed bat and a lesser short-tailed bat, are localized—that is, you will never see one. Like the katipo. And I suppose you could count seals (there are fur seals, sea lions, leopard seals, crab-eater seals, elephant seals, all racing around New Zealand waters, though many were killed off first by the Maori, then by English settlers) and dolphins (nine different species, from the beloved bottlenose dolphin to the rare Hector's dolphin, numbering only between three and four thousand), but seals and dolphins don't really belong to any particular place, do they? Or rather, they belong to the whole ocean, and no country can lay claim to them.

The landscape is benign. The climate is mild. Do I think such a physical environment is good for people? Of course! It makes them benign. This, coupled with a kind of informality, a lack of pretentiousness, is essential to the Kiwi character, and has always been recognized as such. The writer and politician John A. Lee recalled World War I Kiwi soldiers passing a British officer putting a monocle in his eye to assess them. One soldier yelled out: "Yah, you silly bugger, why don't you get another one and stick it up your arse and turn yourself into a periscope." So it goes back at least to the early part of the last century. In the Second World War, a high-ranking British officer complained that Kiwi soldiers did not salute superiors like himself. His New Zealand counterpart said: "Ah, yes, but if you wave to them, they'll wave back." And they did.

*T*oday in New Zealand, even the politicians are benign. I looked in the local telephone directory for Phil Goff and called his number. He is the foreign minister of New Zealand. Also the minister for justice. "What should I call you?" I asked.

"What? Are you kidding? My name is Phil."

"Phil, I am writing a book about New Zealand. Would you come down to our house on the bay and have lunch?"

"Sure, why not?" he said. And he did. I kid you not. Imagine his American counterpart, Colin Powell, the secretary of state, coming down to lunch at your house, just to be nice.

I remember eating lunch with my best friend at the college where he was teaching, All Souls College at Oxford. There was a man standing behind him during the entire lunch. "My scout," he said apologetically. This was an Oxford euphemism for "servant." Talk about pompous. Well, that sort of thing never happens in New Zealand. Arrogance is far removed from the Kiwi character. Phil Goff, it seems to me, exemplifies what is best about New Zealand: Egalitarianism is not just a fantasy, it is partly realized. He was not just being a politician when he chatted with everybody who happened to drop by our house on the beach that day. (On any given day a dozen people might wander by, some whom I know, some whom I just meet then.) He does not stand on ceremony because there is no ceremony on which to stand in this country. In America, he is given bodyguards; here that would be a joke. No New

Zealander talks down to anyone, he explained to me, because "when you're as little as us, there's no one to talk down *to*."

*B*ut there are some drawbacks to the concept of an egalitarian society, though the ideal is a good one. They have what they call here the "tall poppy syndrome"—that is, if you stand out too markedly, you will be cut down. The term *public intellectual* is not used in New Zealand. I am not sure it is even understood. When I first arrived and asked people about them, they stared back at me blankly. What was I talking about? Nobody would call him- or herself an intellectual here—that would be "skiting," basically bragging about yourself. But in America there are many people who are considered public intellectuals, that is, people who write about ideas for a large audience: The late great I. F. Stone was always my favorite, but today there is Christopher Hitchens, whom nobody loves; or someone you have to force yourself to read, like Susan Sontag; or somebody you mostly agree with even if it's boring, like Noam Chomsky; or about whom you can become rapturous and applaud, like the courageous Michael Moore; or Gore Vidal, who writes so well. Canada has them, too, sublime novelists like the late Margaret Lawrence or Margaret Atwood, or in England, the hateful Martin Amis, or the wonderful John Pilger in Australia, or the pompous French intellectuals, all unreadable, like Bernard Levy or the unbearable Derrida. Chile has them (Ariel Dorfman), as do Germany (Hans Magnus Enzensberger) and Holland (Harry Mulisch). India has many (such as the formidable Arundhati Roy), and Italy has them (the great Primo Levi, and

Umberto Eco, Pasolini, Fellini, Moravia, Calvino), and Ireland has an entire population of them. Just about every country on earth has them. Except New Zealand.

I am talking about people who take a stance about social issues and write for a general audience. They write about ideas and they write on many different topics and they have very strong views, and there are always a lot of people who disagree violently, and so you get a lot of public ferment. Sometimes the topic is in the news, like the huge debate in the 1960s over Hannah Arendt's book *Eichmann in Jerusalem,* or the later public furor over Daniel Jonah Goldhagen's *Hitler's Willing Executioners,* or the debate over the effects of television on young children, or whether there is such a thing as hate speech and should it be regulated, or of course the war on Iraq.

It is not that such things are never written about in New Zealand; they are. There are intelligent social commentators (people like Jane Kelsey, Sandra Coney, Michael King, James Belich, Gordon McLauchlan, Nicky Hager, Brian Easton), but what they write is rarely the topic of general conversation. Ideas do not fire New Zealanders. They want to get their hands on something and do something physical to it. They like to be able to touch something and then fix it. They like wire, especially number 8 wire, with which Kiwis seem to be able to build or fix anything. It is wonderful to be around a New Zealander in an emergency. They are great next-door neighbors, too. You never want to be in the bush without a Kiwi along. Never go on a bike ride without one because she will fix your puncture and send you in the right direction as soon as you get lost. (I know, we did.) But just don't expect them to sit down in your library with you for a few hours and talk about the books. It would embarrass them. There are obviously many people who can, but even they won't. It's just not a Kiwi thing.

I have thirteen thousand books in my house, with different rooms for volumes on the Holocaust, feminism, animals, psychiatry, antipsychiatry, memory, dreams, evolution, Darwin, Freud—a kind of history of my own varied career in and out of the university. I love my library, and would relish the opportunity to talk about it with somebody here. *Dream on.* They come, they glance at the books, they look over at me with a raised eyebrow, then ask some inanity like "Have you read all these books?"—but they won't really talk about them. They will, however, comment on how well made the shelves are, how thick, what fine wood. They feel them, examine them, and figure out how it was done. They admire good work, but are embarrassed to be seen admiring something as blatantly of the mind as a good library.

There is another negative aspect to this modesty. It is hard for a New Zealander to make an outlandish compliment. When a recent visitor to our house met Leila for the first time, she said to a mutual friend: "Does he know he is married to a goddess?" She was an American. No Kiwi would say such a thing. To enthuse over a person is bad manners, somehow improper. I asked Witi Ihimaera, New Zealand's most famous Maori author (he wrote the book upon which the film *Whale Rider* was based), how his parents reacted to his soaring fame. "Mutedly," he explained, for Maoris are not Jews to qvell over their children's success. No "Help! Help! My son the doctor is drowning" for Maoris or for Kiwis in general.

New Zealand is now my home. Can it be my home the way it is "home" to somebody who has lived here all his or her life? I am not sure. I remember going to Israel to attend a conference with my best friend at the time, Charles Hanly, a professor of philosophy at the University of Toronto, and a psychoanalyst. The last evening we spent walking along the boardwalk in the seaside town of Netanya. There was a warm breeze, people were laughing in the streets, children playing, and the sea was warm and blue. It was a tropical night, and we stayed out very late, drinking in the sights and enjoying the beauty. The next day we returned to Toronto. It was the middle of fall and at the corner of Bloor and Bathhurst, a cold wind carried dirty newspapers in the air. Chuck turned to me and said: "Are you thinking what I'm thinking?"

"Yes," I replied, "how hard it is to leave warm, friendly Israel"—as long as you are a Jew, not a Palestinian—"and come back to this cold, *goyish* country."

"No," he corrected (after asking what *goyish* meant), "I meant how good it is to be home!"

I guess for him Toronto (and Canada in general) was home in a way it could not be for me, though I had lived there nearly eight years. These sights, so alienating to me, spelled home for him; they were familiar, and they spoke of his childhood. What in me awakened dismay (*what am I doing here?*) in him awakened nostalgia. He did not judge these sights, he missed them.

So in what sense can I call New Zealand home after having lived here just three years? The answer came to me the other day when somebody told me he "owned" the river in front of his house. That was pretty funny. I was with a Maori friend, and he thought it was funny, too. How do you *own* a river? Come to think of it, how you do own any property? The huge rock in your backyard? The giant tree in the front yard? The pond on your land? The land itself? It will all be here long after you and I are gone. We lay claim to things that cannot be laid claim to. These permanent natural objects mock us. I don't know about the rock, but I am pretty sure the tree has a life of its own, a biography in fact. The pond is teeming with life, over which I have no control. The emotions that these natural objects arouse in me are truly mine. Those I own. Those belong to me. But those same natural objects arouse different emotions in other people. And those emotions are theirs to own as well. It doesn't matter if they have lived there all their life or just a day; they can still feel and be made to feel by their natural surroundings. Home is where we feel most deeply. If a visitor from Tibet is walking along "my" beach, and has feelings that arise because of what he sees there, he can take those feelings wherever he likes and they will always be his. When he revisits this place, it could be home to him if it brings him home to himself, to his own feelings.

When we lose that connection, when we no longer feel

anything for a place, we can say that it is no longer home. The greatest loneliness is being where you feel you do not belong. It is an odd sensation and can overcome a man (I speak deliberately here) just about anywhere. I have felt it many times. I felt it in Toronto during the long, cold, gray winter. My daughter was less than two and woke up very early every morning, before five. My wife Terri had been breast-feeding all night and desperately needed some rest, so by 6 AM I would take Simone out for an early-morning walk in the still-sleeping city. She was wrapped from head to toe in blankets, and I had gloves and earflaps. We would walk for two hours. It seemed the city never awoke and that we were the only people there. "I am with my daughter, just where I should be," I kept saying. Yet I had a deep sense of not belonging there, right there where I was, in a freezing northern city. I spoke to nobody in the streets—there was no one to speak to. This was the early 1970s, and there were no bustling cafés, no street life that early in the morning (though we were in the middle of the city). The loneliness would overcome me each morning, but then I met a group of women who also brought their children out early. It got worse. They were all Canadians and were quiet, not all that expressive or overly enthusiastic about anything. Nobody spoke much. I thought they might all be lonely, too. Now I cannot help wondering if all of us, if the whole city, were not suffering from SAD, seasonal affective disorder. It happens in places where there is not enough light—where the winter season drags on too long and the spirit is crushed by darkness.

Our bodies were not designed to rarely see the sun. Or maybe it is our souls that were not so designed. I hungered for light, for sunshine, for the sound of birds and the movement of warm water, for spring. When I was invited to Berkeley, California, to give a lecture, I was ecstatic. For a few days I felt like I belonged somewhere. I did. I was from California, or at least had spent most of my life there, and I was going home.

At the time, of course, while I was in analytic training, I looked for psychopathology everywhere, especially in myself. (It was a variant on the medical-student syndrome: You find illnesses you have just learned about everywhere—after all, if you are a hammer, the saying goes, you look for a nail.) Depression fascinated me. I was sure I was depressed. Not the full-blown depression that psychiatrists like to call a "clinical" depression (makes it sound more medical, hence added prestige); just a mild form of sadness that seemed to last as long as the interminable winter.

Now I think it was something different that I was experiencing. Because the loneliness of not being where you think you should be has overcome me since, even in much warmer climates. Even in the Berkeley summer.

I did return to Berkeley, for what I thought was permanent residence. It lasted for nearly twenty-five years, so it was more permanent than anything else I had experienced in my life. I awoke as if from a dream the minute I saw the Pacific Ocean and hiked the Berkeley hills. My sadness lifted like mist from a mountain. But I still found myself feeling something similar to what I had felt in Canada. It was still the sense *You do not belong here.* Wherever *here* was.

Maybe going home is only a metaphor, for all of us. Home might be nothing more than a feeling of being where we should be. I feel now that I am where I belong, and I would like to take the rest of this book to explain why.

chapter 2

The Joy of Living Here as Opposed to There: Comparing Cultures

I have just sat down and counted the different countries I have lived in. The list is longer than I remembered. In chronological order, usually for at least a year, I have lived in: the United States (Los Angeles and Berkeley, California; Kailua on Oahu, Hawaii; Cambridge and Boston, Massachusetts; Providence, Rhode Island—some of these places are almost like different countries in themselves), Switzerland (in the mountains above Lausanne), Uruguay (Montevideo), France (Paris and Cannes), India (Mumbai, or Bombay as it was then known, Calcutta, Pune), Sri Lanka (Colombo, Peradeniya), Italy (Viareggio), Canada (Toronto), Germany (Munich and Berlin), England (London), and now, of course, New Zealand. Moreover, I have traveled extensively throughout Europe, Asia, and the Middle East.

I was always a little bit suspicious about "national character" and generalizations that began with "All Americans are . . . ," or "The French have a tendency to . . . ," or "Italians always prefer . . . ," or "Of course Germans are known for . . . ," or "The English never . . ." On the other hand, when you go from country to country, it becomes impossible to avoid making some of these generalizations yourself at least in your own head, even if you are too nervous to express them to others. For while it may be nothing more than a vast generalization, it is nonetheless obvious to everyone that the English are more reticent in social behavior than the Italians, and the Germans more dour than the French. Indeed, such generalizations are no less common today. As I write, the Pulitzer Prize–winning journalist David Halberstam has just published a book, *Defining a Nation,* in which he enlisted thirty-six distinguished American writers to examine *The Remarkable Circumstances That Shaped the American Character.* And not too long ago Geoffrey Gorer's *Explaining English Character* and Luigi Barzini's *The Italians* were immensely popular. Such studies go back to Thucydides, an Athenian aristocrat who wrote *The History of the Peloponnesian War* in 430 BCE, perhaps the first historian to leave out gods or fate and account for history through national character and its relation to our tendency to war. Alexis de Tocqueville's classic book *Democracy in America* is considered a timeless study of the American character even though he traveled to the United States thirty years before the Civil War. The same is true of Madame de Staël on the German national character. Indeed, it is probably safe to say that no country is without a study on the national character of its people: I have read books about the national character of Canada, Japan, Israel, India, Holland, Spain, Mexico, Russia, and many other countries. Most of these books are, I admit, often breathtakingly obvious, yet the impulse to understand a foreign culture is not trivial.

*H*aving lived in all those places, if I had the choice—and come to think of it, I *do* have the choice, because I am a writer and can write from any place in the world—would I live somewhere else as opposed to here? I would not. Let me briefly give my own, very personal, reasons.

ENGLAND. I found living in London intellectually exciting: We were close to Regents Park and amazing old libraries. I wanted to meet various people whose books I had long admired and whom I knew to be living in London, the novelist Fay Weldon (her novel *Therapy* resonated with my book *Against Therapy*), the philosopher Mary Midgley whose books, including *Animals and Why They Matter*, I treasured above most other books; the former head of the RSPCA, the psychologist Richard Ryder, the first man to name the important concept of "speciesism" (treating our own species as more important than any other—in other words, a form of racism, or at the very least, prejudice); the leading expert on the domestication of animals, Juliet Clutton-Brock from the Museum of Natural History; the classical scholar Richard Sorabji, whose book on the way the ancient world treated animals I found to be a model of its kind; the leftwing Darwinian biologists Steven and Hilary Rose, whose wonderful book *Alas Poor Darwin: Arguments Against Evolutionary Psychology* had just come out; Desmond Morris, the celebrated author of *The Naked Ape*; Stephen Clarke; Jonathan Glover, the philosopher from London University who lived in the house where Sylvia Plath killed herself; and many others. I would call and everyone graciously agreed to spend an afternoon with me. The intellectual stimulation was nearly perfect. The price, though, was steep: London was crowded, expensive, and dirty. The winter seemed endless and relentless. Life here had to be lived primarily indoors. By the end of the season it was getting to me, and our family was eager to leave. The final blow came, I think, when some friends visiting from Germany were told their infant was not welcome in the restaurant where they chose to eat. "We just don't like kids," explained the owner blandly, and not a head turned. It was true: London was not a child-friendly city. Leila is a pediatrician and her whole life is dedicated to children, and since we had a deeply held philosophy of child-friendliness above all other values, this was too much for us. So we left.

Rereading this section, I realize how narrow our own little interests are and how circumscribed are our lives. Imagine dismissing England in a few paragraphs, as I have just done, based on a few mostly accidental encounters and on a limited set of interests. I am somewhat embarrassed, but don't know of any alternative. We *all* live our lives in more or less narrow confines, and the true citizen of the world has yet to be born. How little we know about *anything*, I suddenly realize. "Tell me everything you know about eels," my son Ilan asked me yesterday, and in a few minutes I had come to the very limits of my knowledge. I simply knew nothing else. (Thank God for the Internet!) "What happened in Zimbabwe when it ceased to be

Rhodesia?" Leila asked this morning, and again I realized how quickly I could exhaust my tiny store of knowledge. I was stumped. Yet I consider my own interests to be broad. The key word though, is *interest*. My knowledge is circumscribed, while my enthusiasm knows no bounds!

GERMANY has always been problematic for me, and Berlin particularly so. I speak the language, but I find it harsh, and there are so many echoes of the Holocaust even in the words themselves. When you ride the subway, a voice comes through at every stop: "*Aussteigen!*" You hear words like *heraus, Selektion,* and *Fuehrer* in everyday speech. It is not a pretty reminder. This is purely psychological and can be countered. Far more insidious are the parties where everyone over eighty raises questions in your mind: *What did you do? Where were you? What did you know?* Asking such questions often leads to highly embarrassing situations, unpleasant for both parties. When my partner at the time was invited to spend a year at the Institute for Advanced Studies in Berlin, I was told by Germans, but also by some Americans, that my constant comments about the Holocaust were in poor taste, especially as I was a guest in a German university. There was outrage when I invited a Chilean scholar who had been a pupil of Heidegger, and who was the first to discover in detail Heidegger's Nazi connection. That, too, was in poor taste. Asking about the role of German psychiatry in the Holocaust was also in poor taste. I could do no right. As a Jew, I began to feel distinctly unwelcome and ill at ease. I was in the land of the perpetrator. Of course I met wonderful Germans, people whose lives were dedicated to fighting all forms of fascism and who, had they been alive at the time, would I am sure have fought against Nazism as well. But I never met a single member of any kind of resistance within Germany itself. Such people are rare. (Most were killed, and there were not a lot to begin with; Germany was never Denmark, Bulgaria, or even Italy.) Something about being in Germany did not feel right. Now, it is perfectly true that Germans do more research on the Holocaust than anywhere else except Israel; the quality is very high, but the analysis, the moral stance, is often extremely underdeveloped, as if that aspect were of no interest to them. I suspect they find it rather embarrassing to take on any kind of moral or ethical tone. This is obviously not the case in Israel. When I was in Germany, I was conducting research that would have been extremely difficult to do anywhere else, so I needed to be there, but the thought that I could actually settle down and live in Germany filled me with horror.

When, some years later, I married Leila, a German doctor, I was relieved to find that the thought also filled *her* with horror, so it was not a choice we ever had to make.

Of course not everybody who goes to Germany for any length of time is obsessed with the Holocaust, and German history is not confined entirely to that dark period. My own interests do not define a country, I realize. So many vital young people in and out of the Green party in Germany are doing wonderful things for the environment and for human rights. What I don't know would of course fill many more books than the one I happen to be writing!

Moreover, like the English, the Germans are generally child-unfriendly. Several times when we got on a bus with our two small children, the bus driver shouted at us because we were having trouble getting the jogging stroller up the stairs. Nobody made eye contact to indicate they thought he was out of line; on the contrary, they looked sympathetic to him. I guess they are used to this.

Finally, I must note that outside the major cities, I would not want to be a dark-skinned person. The extreme right, neo-Nazis, may be a small minority, but they are an active one, and there have been many stabbings and attacks on Africans and Turks and other minorities based on race and ethnic origin. Even in the big cities, I remember asking the Turkish owner of one of the many fast-food eateries selling falafel and shawarma some questions about his life in Cologne, where we were. He told me that I was the first person in three years who had asked him a question in his shop. The Germans simply did not acknowledge his existence as a person, and he was only saving enough money for the day he could return home. This feeling is widespread among the Turkish community in Germany. There is no feeling that they are welcome by the local population, and indeed they are not.

FRANCE is the land where my father was born, and I speak the language fluently. In some sense, I feel right at home in Paris. I love the open markets, the streets, the secondhand-book stores, and the parks. I love the feel of everyday life there. But when I read current French intellectual books, I am in an alien country where, even though I can understand the words, I have no idea what they are talking about. Or rather, I think I do know, and it appalls me. Lacan, Derrida, Kristeva, even Foucault, are for me a great chore, not to say bore. Willfully obscure, it is almost impossible to penetrate the jargon, and when you do you wonder why you bothered. Yet these writings entirely captivate the French—whose bookstores are given over to this pretentious drivel. There are of course exceptions (Alain Finkielkraut, or Pierre Vidal-Naquet's books on Holocaust denial, which are superb), but they really are the exceptions. The intellectual climate, and there is such a thing, is sadly one of obscurantism and pompous intellectual vapidity. The vast number of psychoanalytic books published every year add zero to the sum of knowledge. They are a waste of paper and should never have been published.

"Such arrogance," I have been told the few times I had the courage to state my real views. I am convinced, though, that I am right, and therefore I have no business staying in the country for long because *these* are the current ideas, the ones that matter. I could call them fashionable, but that would not be quite fair. They have in fact already withstood the test of time. Derrida and others have been around long enough for people to have made up their minds about them. They are icons of French intellectual thought. *I* am the one out of step. Time to leave.

AMERICA. *Sigh.* I am an American, and when I was in Germany, England, France, I felt it. I was always relieved to meet (some of) my fellow countrymen. I like the openness, the enthusiasm, the friendliness, even if it was not always deep. I liked somebody I just met telling me his or her life story. But recently I have felt that politics have become divisive, and the materialism that was never far from the surface now seems public policy. (The only other place I have been to where shopping is practically a national sport was Dubai.) To stay in America seemed some form of complicity. It is not; I know, for one of the great things about America is our First Amendment rights; thousands of Americans protest and express their opinions on a daily basis, many via the Internet, but there is also the *danger* of being a dissenter in America, something quite remote from New Zealand (where nobody who disagrees with government policy need ever feel threatened). Nobody would ever stop you in the street and try to pick a fight with you because of your views, no matter how high-profile they were.

I wanted out, I wanted away. Of course it was not just recent history. I am ashamed that in a current issue of the prestigious intellectual magazine *Commentary,* an author mocked the request of several African American lawyers that Americans consider paying reparations for slavery, as if this idea were too absurd for commentary. In fact, it is a highly reasonable and understandable request. Slavery continues to have a deep and negative impact on the lives of almost all African Americans. I don't know any reasonable person who believes that black Americans are treated the same as white Americans. Speaking of which, the worst off are African American children, who live below the poverty line in such enormous numbers that it is a scandal of international proportions. Indeed, the level of child poverty in general is increasing in America, and it is an intolerable blot of shame on the entire country. More than a quarter of all children in America live below the official poverty line, and a staggering 50 percent of all African American children do so. Think what that means, when the official poverty threshold in 2002 for a family of four was only $18,370 U.S. dollars a year! Imagine four people trying to live on that small amount of money. It is nearly impossible. Hence the enormous number of homeless people in America, the highest anywhere. For example, while there are no reliable estimates on the total number of homeless people who live where they can on the streets of India's large metropolises of Delhi, Mumbai, and Calcutta and in the smaller cities and towns, that number could easily exceed two million. Yet the U.S. National Law Center on Homelessness and Poverty estimated some *three* million men, women, and children were homeless in the United States for at least some part of 2002, more even than in India. While the numbers are not so high in Europe, in the last few years I have noticed more and more of them; for example, at the main train station in Berlin, where I had not seen them when I was there years before. I have not once seen a homeless person in New Zealand. Somebody who cannot afford to buy or live in a house is entitled to state housing.

I had loved many things about other countries where I had lived. The South American joie de vivre was very appealing to me. There was hardly a moment in Argentina when a party was not either happening or about to happen. South Americans were even more personal and personable than North Americans. You could feel the warmth in the very air you breathed. But Argentina was always in a state of crisis, politically speaking, and this lent living there a certain anxious quality. I was there before the junta, but I don't know how anyone survived under those circumstances.

Italy has some of the same advantages of South America: lively, warm, friendly, and sunny. I love Italy and could easily imagine living in Rome. But whenever I talk to people who actually have lived in Rome, they emphasize how easy it is in the imagination but how difficult in reality. If you were born in Rome, it is easy; if you come from elsewhere, the frustrations begin to undermine your pleasure in living in this fun-filled, sun-soaked city. Too much red tape, too many regulations, too little efficiency. I have read enough to be convinced.

India? Well, of course my time there was fascinating, perhaps more fascinating than any other place I have visited or lived. I became immersed in India in a way I probably could not do in any other country. I knew the ancient language and had studied the ancient culture of both Hinduism and Buddhism more deeply than I had studied anything else at the time. But the ethnic tensions got to me. How could I live in a country where the majority (Hindus) wanted to kill and often did kill the minority (Muslims)? It would be like living in Israel, which in some ways *ought* to be my home, as it was the home of both my mother and my father. I felt it, too, when I would visit. This is *home*, I would think. But then I would talk to people, ordinary Israelis, and I would come to the realization that I was profoundly out of step. Nobody would admit that the Palestinians were badly treated, that even Israeli Arabs were considered second-class citizens precisely because they were Arabs. It was intolerable. Living there, the tension, the fear, the shame, would have eaten away at me. It could not be my home.

Bali? How much I loved the island! It offered everything: extraordinary physical beauty, a people with great friendliness, enormous delicacy; it was also perhaps the single most child-friendly country I had ever visited. I liked the food; in fact I liked everything about Bali, even the fact that Hinduism, which I had once taught at the university, was the dominant religion. It offered just about everything a place could offer, and I once seriously considered moving there. I could learn the language easily (a lot of Sanskrit loan words!), and I would enjoy doing so. True, I would always remain an outsider to the culture, but this status was not one the friendly Balinese looked down upon. I was never treated with contempt. But I never felt entirely safe there, probably because Bali was not an independent country. It was part of Indonesia, and Indonesia would always be a dangerous place for a Jew to live. I think had Bali been its own country, that is where I would most like to live. Moreover, while we were there, there was an outbreak of dengue fever. When our son Ilan came down sick, we became very frightened. The feeling of being medically unsafe was palpable and one I do not want to repeat. With all my criticisms of

Western medicine (where prevention is given short shrift in favor of high-tech fixes)—and they are considerable—I often feel privileged to live where just such medicine is available when you need it. Hypocrisy? Perhaps.

*T*his profound *dis*-ease, in England, in Germany, in France, in America, and just about everywhere else, was not something I have ever felt in New Zealand. It is hard to describe and even harder to explain the ease with which life is lived here, and not just by me. Perhaps it is because the more glaring faults of the other countries are absent here: The government is relatively benign, unlike America; intellectual life, such as it is, is not fraudulent as in France; the history of New Zealand is not horrific, as is the history of Germany; the cities are not crowded, dangerous, dirty, or expensive, the way London is. I make it sound a little bit like Canada, I know. And truth to tell, New Zealand is much like Canada: somewhat dull, slightly lackluster, a bit behind the times, lacking in a certain sense of colorfulness, and yet decent, reliable, kindly, honest. If Vancouver had more sunshine, I would consider living there. If Toronto were in the tropics, I would definitely think it worth considering. But when you take into account that New Zealand has all the better traits of Canada, and yet is an island set in the Pacific Ocean and is, in many ways, a Polynesian island culture, you become suddenly aware that you are living in a most remarkable place.

*I*slands. They have always fascinated me, just as they fascinate many people. Of course, in some sense, every spot on earth is an island—sooner or later you come to the end of land and to the beginning of an ocean. But there is something about an island whose size is manageable, whose tips can be visited by car in a reasonable amount of time, that gives you, or maybe I should only speak for myself here, a sense of enormous pleasure. In this respect New Zealand is the perfect size. I can remember feeling island fever when I lived for a year on Oahu, on the windward side of the island (in Kailua, near Lanikai), in the state of Hawaii. It was physically glorious there, and the weather was as close to perfect as I could imagine. And yet, because you could basically drive right around the entire island in less than a day, I began to feel hemmed in, enclosed, and trapped. It made me nervous that I was beginning to see the same thing over and over: *I have been over this same road now many times.* Suddenly I would panic at the thought: *There is nothing new to see.* Nor was this just a misperception. It was actually true. I had seen everything there was to see on the island: driven every road, taken every hike, and visited every beach. *Help, I am in prison!* I was not, of course, I know, but the feeling of smallness was an actual physical sensation. I could not shake it. I needed to get off the island. It was not entirely psychogenic panic, either; it felt more physical, as if I had a natural home range, and that range was significantly larger than the space I now found myself in. It was almost as if I were wearing clothes that were too tight. I needed a change. I needed to be elsewhere. Leila sometimes has that feeling about New Zealand. It was nice when we lived in London to be able to go to Paris for the weekend at the last minute. Every month or so, we were off to the rest of Europe. Here we often stay on the island for nearly a year. Leila then feels that same itch, that same dissatisfaction. She wants to be elsewhere. But I don't think this is peculiar to islands. When I lived in Toronto, come March all I could think about was getting somewhere sunny and warm. I felt that way in Berlin as well, and added to my discomfort was the desire to get away from German culture. Like so many others who lived there before me, from Goethe on, I longed to be in Italy!

New Zealand does not give me that sensation. Oh, of course I want to leave, several times a year, but I would want that wherever I lived in the world. That is in my blood. My father told me I came from old desert stock—from Uzbekis who lived in tents, nomads who had to travel or die. The old Hanseatic League motto impressed me always: *Navigare necesse est; vivere non necesse.* "It is more important to sail than to live." But my need for exploration, for something new almost every day, is easily satisfied in New Zealand. I love nothing better than to get into our Volvo Cross Country with our two boys and my adventurous wife, and set off for parts unknown. Once a year we head south, for example, to the tip of the South Island. It is a long trip. It takes several weeks and is fascinating in every respect. We see remarkable trees, hear amazing birds, see waterfalls, take walks in parks where we are practically the only people. We are often alone on the road for miles and miles. *Unspoiled* is the word that comes to everyone's mind when driving around New Zealand, and it is the right word. This is unspoiled country. Unspoiled the way the Grand

Canyon is spoiled. I loved driving through Zion National Park in Utah in the United States, but I hated driving at five miles an hour because there were literally hundreds of cars in front and behind me. Visiting the Grand Canyon can make you feel like an ant. Wherever you are, you are part of a vast crowd. The physical beauty cannot be denied, but the means of enjoying it has become more or less out of everyone's reach. When I was still a child, this was not so. I remember trips across America taken with my family fifty years ago where the feeling I now get in New Zealand was dominant. Back then, we were often alone. In fact, I remember feeling lonely, in a cozy, pleasant kind of way. Were we the only ones in the country? I wondered. Now I realize that there are still *some* places like this left in America, but they are becoming less easy to find, whereas in New Zealand just about *everywhere* is like this (except Queenstown, my least favorite place, despite its spectacular beauty, because it so resembles an American resort). It cannot last, of course, and writing this book could perhaps contribute to its inevitable despoliation, its plunder, yet I feel it would be an act of atrocious selfishness on my part to maintain the secrecy of this once best-kept secret in the world. Why should I decide that I alone, or me and my family and my friends, are the only ones entitled to enjoy this extraordinary country?

Why should the fact of merely being born in New Zealand entitle anyone to be among the few who are privileged to live here? Why not share the bounty? In a 1975 book, *Crops and Man*, the late Jack Harlan, perhaps America's most distinguished botanist, wrote that "man is by definition the first and primary weed under whose influence all other weeds have evolved." I like the idea of humans as the urweed, the über-weed. Displacement is in our very nature: We push our way into a land and remove, deliberately or not, other species, plants and animals alike. Humans displace other humans. We are in a constant state of elbowing our way into a place we were not intended to inhabit. We conquer, we ravage, we destroy, and once in a while we learn, usually despite ourselves, how to live in relative peace with species who were already there (but who themselves almost certainly displaced an even earlier inhabitant). Nobody, it would seem, is immune to the colonizing disease. Surely it makes sense to control this impulse, to attenuate it, to do everything in our power to diminish its impact. But we need a sense of humility both for those who came before us and for those who will come later. If we have just managed to slip in under whatever limits have been imposed, should we not express some generosity for those who might wish to do the same? It might well be that too many people in a small country can make it feel crowded. But New Zealand is a large country—almost everywhere we drive, we see miles and miles of empty spaces, places where entire European countries could fit and hardly be noticed. In any event, it would be the height of immodesty to believe that any single book would have an appreciable effect on immigration figures into New Zealand. If a few like-minded souls read this book and decide that they, like us, wish to apply for immigration, I for one welcome them with open arms. True, the beach I now look upon could not accommodate many more people than are already living nearby. But most Aucklanders do not wish to live in a place such as this, where they cannot drive up to their house in a car. They do not, as I do, want to carry their garbage up a long steep path to reach the road. They do not relish the isolation. Some people would rather hear traffic than birds. I love this place, but not everybody does. One of my great pleasures, though, is to show it to others in the hope that they, too, will see what I have fallen in love with here.

chapter 3

Australia Versus New Zealand

*R*estlessness. Some have it, some don't. I do. Always have, probably always will. In my defense, however, is the fact that almost all animals (and humans, after all, are animals, too) have a home territory, a space that they consider important to their well-being. They like to patrol the borders, visit favorite spots, check for intrusions, and otherwise gloat over their good fortune in having a well-maintained area to live in. Some animals, such as wolves, can have territories that even by human standards are vast. For example, in Alaska, the winter range for wolves has been estimated to be from forty square miles for a pair to five thousand square miles for a pack of ten wolves.

Most humans have home territories much smaller than those of wolves. Some, a few of us, like me, have even larger ones. I seem to need the entire world as my home territory. After a while, usually about three months, I grow restless, feeling the urge to travel, to be somewhere else. Living in New

Zealand, that somewhere else turns out to be, more often than not, Australia, since it is a mere fifteen hundred miles away, a short distance compared to flying to Los Angeles (more than six thousand miles), not to mention a three-hour trip as opposed to thirteen!

When I arrive in Australia, I am immediately struck with how different it feels from New Zealand. I was in Melbourne recently, and I felt grateful to be in a city of nearly four million people. The shopping was fantastic, the restaurants were wonderful, and there were whole streets devoted to different ethnic groups: a street for the Turkish population, one for the Vietnamese, an Italian section, and a Greek section. There are more survivors of the Holocaust living in Australia than anywhere else in the world except Israel, so there is a vivid Jewish presence in the city. All of this offers a stark contrast with Auckland. So I shopped, and I ate, and I mixed. And five days later, I began to miss Auckland. It was not just home calling me back, though. I recognized that I had become pleasantly addicted to physical beauty, and that such was lacking in Melbourne (though certainly not Sydney). Melbourne is flat and gray. Even the sea around Melbourne appears flat and gray, like the seas of Northern Europe. There is something dreary about the city. The soul is lovely but the body leaves much to be desired. It is just not a beautiful city. To some people, that matters less than to me. I could not live there. Trees are not nearly as lush and as rich as they are in Auckland. On the other hand, you often see rainbow lorikeets sitting in them, and that is one of the glorious sights of the world.

I began to miss seeing the volcanic island I see from my window, the one I am looking at now as I type these words. The wind is blowing hard, and there are huge whitecaps in the sea. The boats moored in front of our house are bobbing up and down like corks. The sun is bright—the clouds look like little white marbles in the sky. And that island, that green, grass-filled soft island, just beckons to me! The waves rolling into our beach, the many islands off in the distance, lush volcanic peaks visible everywhere, it gets under your skin, this much beauty, it really does. Who would not miss it? Does it matter who your ancestors were? I don't even know the name of my great-grandfather. I know he came from Uzbekistan and had an immense kabbalah library (which I partially inherited, but gave to a library in Israel), but that is pretty much the limit of my knowledge. I don't really know if it matters to a country where the people originally came from. It has been argued that Australians are more lively than New Zealanders because most Australians are descended from Irish criminals, whereas the New Zealanders came from Scottish farmers. I would say this is nonsense except it does not seem to be entirely wrong.

The similarities between New Zealand and Australia, to an outsider, are positively startling: The accent is hard to differentiate; there is a certain roughness to the male characters that is a source of pride; the egalitarian spirit is very much alive in both places; pomposity is pretty much absent. At the same time, both countries have, in the eyes of many outsiders, a similar cultural cringe; a deep-seated mistrust of intellectual activity; a certain nostalgia for the "mother country"; provincialism;

geographic isolation, though in a country as vast as Australia, this matters less than it does in New Zealand. Australia has a much greater diversity of people than does New Zealand. When I lectured in Australia, I found lively, enthusiastic audiences who asked probing questions and debated the topic at hand with great fervor. There was a generosity of spirit in Australia that I find lacking in New Zealand.

The two major cities, Sydney and Melbourne, are very different. I loved Sydney in most respects. How could you not love a city where you are likely to see a magnificently colored parrot every day? Or a great white-crested cockatoo? The trees are overwhelming. I was in a friend's garden looking at a hibiscus plant when I suddenly saw what looked like thousands of tiny shards of sparkling opals. Swarming over the tree were beautiful cotton harlequin bugs, members of the jewel bug family. The females are orange and the males mostly blue-red—I saw literally thousands or hundreds of thousands of them. It was a wonderful experience. At the same time, Sydney is crowded, unsafe, and expensive. It is a big city, a big *international* city.

Something you really don't learn about Australia is just how dangerous it is. You won't learn this from Aussies; they will never tell you. It's too commonplace to them. Imagine this, just for starters: You are in your garden, weeding, right in the middle of Sydney. An ugly, hairy funnel-web spider (there are forty species) the size of a yo-yo takes a bite out of your hand. If you are very young, that single bite is all it takes: You're dead. If not, the bacteria these spiders carry on their fangs will cause your skin to die and your flesh to literally melt away. There is no known antidote. Or the trap-door spider, the size of a fifty-cent piece, feels the vibrations as you walk by, rushes out, and takes a fatal bite out of you. Or you are lucky and just meet the white-tail spider, which bites your hand and causes an ulcerous sore that lasts for months, then leaves a large hole (the bite works like gangrene). Your garden also contains the king brown snake, the most poisonous snake in the world, forty times more venomous than our rattler. Actually, Australia has a hundred poisonous snakes, about a dozen of which rank among the most poisonous on earth. You might step on what you think are some fallen leaves, but discover it is the tiny death adder. Can you guess why they call it that? Equally venomous are taipans, or red-bellied black snakes; you may see twenty of them in half an hour's walk in the hills.

Should you foolishly decide you want to go swimming in Australia, beware the stonefish. It looks like a seaweed-covered stone, but it has a spike. Should you have the misfortune of stepping on it, you're history. We went swimming in a mild-looking bay outside Cairns, where there was a small sign: BOX JELLYFISH. How bad could that be? I was used to swimming in Hawaii and had tangled with many a Portuguese man-of-war. Ha! If the three-foot tentacles of a box jellyfish so much as touch you, the pain is so intense that you scream out of control. Not for long, however, for if you don't get to a hospital soon, you can die. If somebody comes along to take it off you, she is attacked. This jellyfish is so transparent that it's more or less invisible; you don't see it, you just start screaming. Australians would actually rather meet a seagoing saltwater crocodile, all twenty feet of him. These swim between New Guinea and Australia, but will also go thirty miles up a freshwater river. They attack and they kill. Still, they're better than the blue-ringed octopus, common in rock tidal pools around Sydney. Smaller than your hand, when annoyed its blue rings become iridescent, attracting the unsuspecting child. The bite does not hurt, but injects a venom that can lead to total muscular paralysis and the cessation of breathing within minutes. It is the world's most lethal octopus. The problem is that they sometimes wash into the swimming pools that people have built right at the edge of the sea, which fill up with tidal water every day. Total paralysis after the bite means the suffering person cannot speak, though fully conscious. One victim reported her horror at hearing the paramedics saying, "It doesn't look like she's going to make it."

Still, my favorite has got to be the amazing gympie gympie tree. Sound sweet? There are six species. Two grow to 130 feet. They are in Queensland. Don't go there. The hollow plant hair easily breaks off in your skin, injecting a pain-causing toxin that can last for up to one year! Constant, unbearable pain—so extreme that one stricken soldier took his own gun and shot himself. Horses die from the pain. One dried specimen, collected in 1910, is still active. Australian forestry workers carry gloves, antihistamine, and a respirator. The extreme shock of the pain can cause a heart attack and death. You don't even have to touch this tree. You can just be sitting beneath it minding your own business. *Wham!* You're dead.

It is not so different elsewhere in the world. When I was studying Sanskrit I lived in Calcutta for a while. I remember once suggesting that we go on a picnic. My Bengali friends laughed: Are you nuts? Biting ants, mosquitoes the size of B-57s, large scorpions—there was no end to insects and animals who could spoil our life, let alone the picnic. In contrast, *everything* is benign in New Zealand.

When I was traveling in Australia, I was surprised at the number of comments I heard that were overtly racist, especially in Alice Springs and in Darwin, where many indigenous people live. It was the only place I heard the word *abo* used, a denigrating designation more or less equivalent to the American *nigger,* and with equally ugly connotations and historical associations. Not just once, but over and over, people in Alice Springs would say something like "Ah, now your abo, he gets lots of money from the government, but throws it all away because he has no use for money. If you buy him a new car, he makes it look like an old car in a matter of days." "Why would he do that?" "Ah, it's just a cultural thing. The culture does not value material things." I thought perhaps they were making a disguised compliment—after all, what a wonderful thing for a culture to be unconcerned with materialism—but no, they were showing how ignorant these people were. And this in a place surrounded by amazing vestiges of the art and wonder of a marvelous culture: Uluru ("the world's most beautiful rock") is just hours away, and one of the most beautiful spots on earth, long worshiped, understandably, by the indigenous people.

New Zealand is different. The Maori language, after all, is, along with English, the official language of the country (since 1987, by a legislative act), and all signs are in both. You are unlikely to hear derogatory comments about the Maori unless you deliberately look for them. (Of course racism is universal, and New Zealand has its fair share—but it is frowned upon just about everywhere and is therefore rarely expressed to a foreigner such as me.) At the time of European contact, there were probably two hundred thousand Maori. By 1896 this was down to forty-two thousand, the lowest number ever recorded. Yet at the time of the last census, in 2001, this was figure was 526,281—more if one includes people with some Maori ethnicity. In a country of less than four million people, 14 percent are Maori. Of the 120 members of Parliament in New Zealand, 20 are Maori, almost 20 percent. Contrast this with the United States: Of the 535 members of Congress, 435 in the House of Representatives and 100 in the Senate, there are 38 African Americans, *all* in the House; 21 Hispanics, also all in the House; and only 2 Native Americans, one a senator. In 1992 Carol Moseley Braun became the first African American woman to sit in the U.S. Senate, and only the second African American since Reconstruction to be a senator. The black population in America today is thirty-six million, or 13 percent of the population, roughly the same proportion as the Maori in New Zealand. The Native American population (of a total of 281 million Americans as of 2000) is about 2.5 million, just under 1 percent.

*T*he history of harms against indigenous people in Australia is every bit as bloody as the American history of racism and violence against blacks, and is nothing to be proud of. Everyone who saw the amazing film *Rabbit-Proof Fence* by the director Phillip Noyce knows about the attempt on the part of the Australian government to forcibly remove "half-caste" Aboriginal children from their parents to train as domestic servants and as a means of ensuring that the race itself would eventually disappear. "I would not hesitate to separate any half-caste from its aboriginal mother, no matter how frantic momentary grief might be at the time," wrote one "protector." "They soon forget their offspring." He maintained it was just like removing a pup from a bitch. The astonishing thing is that this practice (begun in 1900) continued right up to 1971! At the time, almost no white people protested, or even seemed to care much about the practice. Where is the apology? Australian senator Aden Ridgeway argues passionately for a "need for a formal national apology to the stolen generations to acknowledge and heal the suffering that has been borne by generations of indigenous families as a consequence of removing children from their lands, cultures and families." In fact, the "White Australia Policy" took nearly twenty-five years to erode, and it was really only in 1978 that racism was no longer official government policy. But Australia has still not acknowledged Aboriginal and Torres Strait Islander People (who take their name from the strait that separates the Australian mainland at Cape York from the south coast of Papua New Guinea) as the first people of Australia, even though that is exactly what they are. Aden Ridgeway, the *only* indigenous member of the Australian Federal Parliament, says, "The taking of our lands, our cultures, and our children is a fundamental reason for our current economic disadvantage and socio-political marginalization."

Of course what strikes every visitor immediately about Australia is how vast a country it is. From Sydney to Darwin, for example, is nearly twenty-five hundred miles, like driving across the United States. And how compact, in contrast, New Zealand is. Nearly everything you want to drive to is just hours away. You are out of the city in minutes, whereas we drove and drove in Sydney. While it was all gorgeous, we seemed, hours later, to be making little progress. Australia is also closer to places than is New Zealand. There, you do not have the sense of being in the middle of nowhere. Bali is hours away. So is much of Asia. Australia is much closer to America in sentiment than is New Zealand; Americanization has taken root much more firmly in Australia than it has in New Zealand. The Aussies make endless jokes about their "poor" cousin: "What is the capital of New Zealand?" Answer: "Four dollars."

It is true there is more of an international flavor in Australia than in New Zealand. You have a much greater choice of schools for your children, for example, and many of them are far more progressive than is possible to find here. There is nothing provincial about Sydney or Melbourne, no sense that the clock has stopped or that you have stepped back in time—

something you can easily feel in New Zealand, both for better and for worse.

I love both places. I am glad to be living in New Zealand, but also glad that it is just a short flight away from its bigger, more cosmopolitan relative across the Tasman. I would feel greatly impoverished if I could not visit Australia at least once a year, and many New Zealanders feel the same way, though they seldom say so publicly. The rivalry between the two countries is legendary, but also something tongue-in-cheek. Whatever separates the two people is far less important than their similarities. They might not be one people, but they are certainly close relatives.

chapter 4

Fifty Important Dates in New Zealand History: A Personal Perspective

I call this a personal perspective because about half of the dates I've listed here would readily be acknowledged by just about any New Zealander, and the other half are what strike *me* as important dates, but could easily be contested.

1. c. 1000 CE: Arrival of first Polynesians.

   The Polynesians who first came to New Zealand, either deliberately or by accident, came from either the Cook Islands or the Society Islands (of which Tahiti is one), but they did not remain. (Only the Pacific rat, itself originally from Southeast Asia, stayed behind, to begin the process of extinction of native fauna.) They spoke an Austronesian language, ancestral to New Zealand Maori, and were in other ways similar to the Maori who came later.

2. c. 1350: Mythical arrival of the "great fleet" from Hawaiki.

A catamaran with young people, men and women of childbearing age, who intended to stay, from Rarotonga or Tahiti, or even the Marquesas, containing provisions, including plant material such as the coconut and the sweet potato (kumara), as well as a pregnant dog, arrived in the north of the North Island, on the East Coast. Hawaiki has never been identified, though the name is well known in Eastern Polynesia. The initial human population was no more than two hundred.

3. 1700: Extinction of the moa.

Present in huge numbers when the Maori first arrived, within a short time (in the Coromandel Peninsula, for example, in perhaps a mere five years) these astonishing giant birds, with no evolved fear of humans, were all killed for food. No details about their habits have come down in Maori mythology, suggesting that they were killed so quickly there was no time to record anything at all about them. Since the Maori had no bows and arrows, and no spears, it is likely the birds made no attempt to run away, and were killed at close range with clubs. The word itself is the name for "fowl" in Tahitian. Richard Owen (who coined the term *dinosaur*), the English paleontologist and the greatest comparative anatomist of his time, examined the first moa bone in 1839 and published his announcement of the existence of moa in 1840.

SOURCE: The last word, probably for some time, is the authoritative book by Trevor H. Worthy and Richard N. Holdaway, *The Lost World of the Moa: Prehistoric Life of New Zealand*. Bloomington: Indiana University Press, 2002.

4. 1769: Captain James Cook circumnavigates both main islands; 95 percent of the Maori population is in the North Island.

James Cook's first expedition explored New Zealand in 1769 and 1770 in the *Endeavour*. He stayed six months, then returned for two further visits, in 1773 and 1777 (during which time he released domestic pigs), staying for a total of 328 days. His journals, published already in 1773, remained for years basic reference texts, even for other ships entering the Pacific, and the writings and drawings of men who came with him—Joseph Banks, the Forsters, William Monkhouse—were to prove invaluable, not to mention the first map, remarkably precise and comprehensive, of both islands. His encounters with the Maori people (who thought the ship was a floating island or a giant bird) were by and large positive, primarily because he brought along with him Tupaea, an English-speaking Tahitian priest who was able to understand the language. Cook provided a positive report on abundance of timber, flax, seals, and whales, all of which would be exploited to near extinction in the years to come. Cook introduced the Maori to guns (though he left none behind) and nails, the latter of which were much admired. He also introduced the pathogens that would eventually decimate the Maori population—who had no immunity to them because they were previously unknown to them.

SOURCE: Perhaps the single best source about Captain Cook are his journals, splendidly edited by J. C. Beaglehole, *The Journals of Captain James Cook on His Voyages of Discovery*. 4 vols.: Cambridge University Press for the Hakluyt Society, 1955–69; and the same author's *The* Endeavour *Journal of Joseph Banks, 1768–1771.* 2 vols. Sydney: Angus & Robertson, 1962. They are not easy to find, however. More accessible are the three books by Anne Salmond, *Two Worlds* (1991), *Between Worlds* (1997), and *The Trial of the Cannibal Dog* (2003).

5. 1770: Half of New Zealand's bird species are extinct.
In addition to the moa, the large eagle, a pelican, and several flightless geese died out, along with another twenty bird species. Damage to the environment began the minute people settled in New Zealand. Even apart from humans hunting birds who were friendly rather than flighty, fires set either deliberately or accidentally in the fourteenth century created large tracts of grassland. In the South Island alone, half of the original forest was permanently converted to tussock grassland, with disastrous results for the birds who had lived in the native forests. With the disappearance of the birds, other animals were affected—the lizards who fed on the vegetation, for instance, which in turn depended on the guano of petrels. The disappearance of these pollinators and seed dispersers affected the distribution of other plants and the lives of other animals. The elimination of arboreal geckos by the introduced rat was also the beginning of a negative chain effect.

SOURCE: *The Lost World of the Moa,* and also the splendid book edited by Malcolm McKinnon, *New Zealand Historical Atlas.* Wellington: David Bateman in Association with Historical Branch, Department of Internal Affairs, 1997.

6. 1814: Arrival of Samuel Marsden, the first Christian missionary.
This bluff Yorkshireman, a chaplain in the New South Wales penal colony in Australia, set up the first Church of

England's Church Missionary Society mission in 1814 in the Bay of Islands, a few hours from Auckland. He also introduced horses and cattle. The settlement of three families was a failure, and at least one of the men, Thomas Kendall, a schoolmaster and justice of the peace, confessed that "the sublimity" of Maori ideas had "almost completely turned me from a Christian to a Heathen." By 1822 there was still not a single conversion. The situation changed, however, when the missionaries learned Maori and began translating the Bible, and perhaps, too, because Maori confidence was undermined by the large number of people being killed by European diseases to which they were vulnerable.

SOURCE: Michael King, *The Penguin History of New Zealand*. Auckland: Penguin, 2003. For a biography of Marsden, see A. T. Yarwood, *Samuel Marsden*. Melbourne: Oxford University Press, 1968.

7. 1830s: Sealing and whaling stations are dotted around the coast.

These stations were rough areas (Charles Darwin, visiting the Bay of Islands in the *Beagle* in 1835, described its English residents as "the very refuse of society") where the men treated each other hardly any better than the animals they were hunting to extinction or near extinction. Seals and sea lions were eliminated as breeding species from large areas; the New Zealand fur seal was reduced to relict populations in the South Island. Deep-sea whaling was backed mainly by the Americans and the British. In 1839 there were eighty American whale ships in New Zealand.

The seal was practically the only native mammal in New Zealand.

8. **1835: The Moriori on Chatham Islands, who had given up warfare, are colonized and enslaved by two mainland Maori tribes.**

    The inhabitants of the Chatham Islands (about five hundred miles east of the South Island) were Polynesians who had come from New Zealand at some point in the fourteenth or fifteenth century. Only sixteen hundred in number, they called themselves Moriori (a dialectical version of the word *Maori*). They were a peaceful people, with no concept of an aristocracy, and—what I find astonishing and why I am most interested in this little-known people—they had given up warfare and replaced it with a symbolic hand-to-hand combat that never resulted in serious injury. In 1835 two Maori tribes, Ngati Mutung and Ngati Tama from Wellington, hijacked a ship and invaded the island, killing 10 percent of the inhabitants and enslaving the rest. Curiously, the Moriori are not mentioned in *The Oxford History of New Zealand*.

    SOURCE: The best book is by Michael King, *The Moriori: A People Rediscovered*. Auckland: Penguin, 1989 (rev. ed. 2000).

9. **1820–40: Alcohol is introduced to the Maori.**

    I find this fact interesting because of the devastating effects alcohol has had on the lives of those who had no knowledge of it in their own culture. Maori is one of the few cultures with no indigenous production of any alcoholic beverage. Joseph Banks, the naturalist who traveled with James Cook, said of the Maori: "Water is their universal drink." The Maori called alcohol waipiro, "stinking water." They had no tolerance for it (does anyone?), and a group of Waikato chiefs sent a letter to Parliament in 1856 stating of alcohol: "This is the worst thing hitherto brought to New Zealand."

SOURCE: www.waipiro.org.nz.

10. An Australian "buys" the South Island and Stewart Island for two hundred pounds.

I read this on page 968 of the *Rough Guide to New Zealand*, and found it fascinating, but I could not verify it anywhere else. What the guide says is: "The Australian emancipationist [that is, he wished to emancipate convicts], William Charles Wentworth, had 'bought' the South Island and Stewart Island for a few hundred pounds (the largest private land deal in history, subsequently quashed by government order) and British settlers were already setting sail."

11. 1840: Treaty of Waitangi.

Perhaps the single most important event in New Zealand history. Signed by William Hobson (for the British Crown) and five hundred Maori chiefs, the document promised Maori total control of their lands if they gave up sovereignty to the Crown. The problem was in the translation: Maori has no equivalent to many of the words used in the treaty, so the two texts are almost completely different documents, understood differently by each party. For example, in the English text, the treaty says, "the Crown retains the right of pre-emption over Maori lands." The idea was for the government to buy land from Maori cheaply and to re-sell it to settlers for a high price. The Maori, according to the English understanding of the treaty, were not allowed to sell their own land to anyone but the government, and should the government not be interested, they could not offer it to anyone else. The Maori understood the text to refer to "hokonga" trading. *Hoko* in Maori means to buy or sell; *hokonga* literally means "sale and purchase."

SOURCE: The best book I have read about the treaty is by Claudia Orange, *The Treaty of Waitangi*. Wellington: Allen & Unwin, 1987. See also I. H. Kawharu, editor, *Waitangi: Maori and Pakeha Perspectives of the Treaty of Waitangi*. Auckland: Oxford University Press, 1989.

12. Maori "prophetic" movements.

There were many such movements, the first being the Papahurihia, the name of both the visionary leader and the god. He claimed his people were Hurai, "Jews," and the early Israel of the Bible played a major role in this and subsequent religions of the Maori. The second one was Pai Marire (*pai* means "good"; *marire*, "peace") or Hauhau (winds, breath of life) faith, led by Te Ua in 1862, and his followers called themselves Tiu, "Jews," and preached liberation from oppressors (settlers) by means of war if necessary. The books of Moses were their laws. At its height in 1865, about one-fifth of the total Maori population were Hauhau. Civil war broke out and lasted seven years.

The Pai Marire prisoners were sent to the Chatham Islands, where they became followers of a new faith born there: the Ringatu ("upraised hand," because they do not kneel in submission), led by Te Kooti in 1867. He escaped the island along with 163 men, sixty-four women, and seventy-one children, and led an armed resistance as a formidable guerrilla leader until 1872. He died in 1892, leaving behind a complexly structured church blending Jewish and Christian themes, which is still influential today. The final important movement is the Ratana, named for the prophet Tahupotiki Ratana. Started in 1918, it was based on teachings from two texts: the Bible and the Treaty of Waitangi. He was most concerned with the effects of the 1918 influenza pandemic, which hit Maori seven times harder than the Pakeha (non-Polynesian settlers). By 1926 almost a fifth of the Maori population said they were followers. Ratana made an alliance with the Labour party in 1935, but his real aim was autonomy, not yet achieved. In the 1981 census, Ratana remained the largest indigenous faith and the third largest religion of the Maori after the Anglican faith and Roman Catholicism.

SOURCE: I have used the excellent chapter "Maori Prophet Leaders" by Judith Binney in *The Oxford Illustrated History of New Zealand,* edited by Keith Sinclair. 2nd ed. Auckland: Oxford University Press, 1997. See her remarkable book, *Redemption Songs: A Life of Te Kooti Arikirangi Te Turuki.* Auckland: Auckland University Press, 1995. On Hauhau, see Paul Clark, *Hauhau: The Pai Marire Search for Maori Identity.* Auckland, 1975. On Ringatu, see William Greenwood, *The Upraised Hand or the Spiritual Significance of the Rise of the Ringatu Faith.* 3rd ed. Wellington, 1980. On Ratana, see J. Macleod Henderson, *Ratana: The Man, the Church, the Political Movement.* 2nd ed. Wellington, 1972.

13. 1858: Settlers outnumber Maori. Between 1860 and 1880 the non-Maori population rises from 60,000 to 470,000.

At first Maori were not aware that the coming of the Pakeha could harm them in any way, since they vastly outnumbered the arriving settlers. There were anywhere between one and two hundred thousand Maori living on both islands when the first settlers arrived. Maori were eager for some of the possessions of the Pakeha, and the Pakeha were eager for the land. Maori owned land communally and did not at first understand what "possession" meant in Western terms. One Maori chief, when he saw boatload upon boatload of settlers arriving, fell to his knees on the beach and wept. He foresaw doom.

14. 1858: Beginnings of the Maori King Movement.

The first national hui, or formal assembly, of Maori leaders was called in 1856 at Taupo to counter uncontrolled land sales and the rising power of the settlers. One of the Maori leaders, Wiremu Tamihana of Ngati Haua, pushed for the selection of a Maori king, to counter the power of Queen Victoria: "I do not desire to cast the Queen from this island, but from my piece of land." The first king was an elderly Waikato chief, Potatau Te Wherwhero, who was elected king after a long process involving hundreds of tribes from both the South Island and the North Island, but he died after only two years in office. Still, the movement—called the Kingitanga—was begun and would continue to influence politics in New Zealand thereafter. Potatau was succeeded by his son, Tawhiao, and by 1863 the majority of Maori supported the movement. It was an attempt to stop the grabbing of land by the Crown and by settlers and to achieve some sort of tribal unity. While it ultimately failed in the first goal, it achieved the second.

SOURCE: Alan Ward, *A Show of Justice: Racial 'Amalgamation' in Nineteenth Century New Zealand*. Canberra: Australian National University Press, 1974. Also by Ward, *The Shadow of the Land: A Study of British Policy and Racial Conflict in New Zealand, 1832–1852*. Wellington: Government Printer, 1968. James Belich, *The New Zealand Wars and the Victorian Interpretation of Racial Conflict*. Auckland: Oxford University Press, 1991. Keith Sinclair, *The Origins of the Maori Wars*. Wellington: New Zealand University Press, 1957. See also plate 36 in the *New Zealand Historical Atlas*.

15. 1860–65: Land wars between Pakeha and Maori.

A kind of prewar was started when a chief, Hone Heke, one of the first to sign the Treaty of Waitangi, became disillusioned with the way it was being interpreted. In a symbolic act in 1844, he cut down the British flagpole at Russell (Kororareka as it was then still called). He was defeated by a new governor, George Grey, primarily because he could not unite the Maori on his side. Slowly, however, it became apparent that the settlers and the government wanted Maori land, all of it if possible, and had no intention of respecting the rights, dignity, or mana of the Maori, and even of their king. Maori scholar Ranginui Walker puts it succinctly and well: "The government waged war against the Maori King and confiscated three million acres of land under the New Zealand

Settlement Act of 1863. After the New Zealand Wars, the Maori still held the major portion of the North Island, sixteen million acres to the Crown's ten million acres. From 1867 to the turn of the century, this land was systematically alienated by legal artifice through the operation of the Native Land Court." What Grey wanted was nothing less than an invasion of Waikato, "King Country." He had nearly ten thousand troops at his command. The king's capital, Ngaruawahia, fell, and a major confrontation took place at Orakau. The Maori retreated and the war was officially over, but guerrilla warfare continued for many more years. The armed garrison was finally disbanded in 1885. The war did not become, however, a race war, since many settlers (including the former chief justice, Sir William Martin, as well as Bishop Selwyn and others) supported the cause of the Kingis. While many Maori fought on the government side, it was also clear that they achieved, perhaps for the first time, a unified response, with tribes from the deep south fighting with their Maori brethren in the north. At the end of the war, however, in Waikato alone the area that was finally confiscated came to almost one million acres.

SOURCE: See the chapter "Maori and Pakeha" by M. P. K. Sorrenson in *The Oxford History of New Zealand,* edited by Geoffrey W. Rice. 2nd ed. Auckland: Oxford University Press, 1992. James Belich, *The New Zealand Wars* (see the source note for item 14). See also his chapter, "The Governors and the Maori (1840–1872)," in *The Oxford Illustrated History of New Zealand.* Ranginui Walker's chapter in *The Oxford History* is also excellent. See, too, his *Nga Tau Tohetohe: Years of Anger.* Auckland: Penguin, 1987. See plate 38 of the *New Zealand Historical Atlas.*

16. 1860: The introduction of weasels, ferrets, and stoats (to control rabbits) is recognized as an attempt to "correct a blunder by a crime."

Possum and red deer were also introduced early on, in the hope of cashing in, only to find they had become "pests" (a matter of definition, as is the concept of a "weed"). The Canterbury Acclimatisation Society (founded in 1864) specialized in introducing birds, fish, and mammals to the province where Christchurch is located without any awareness of the far-reaching effects. Even brown trout came to seriously endanger local fish, something of which we have become aware only relatively recently. Introduced plants and trees also colonized native ecosystems and left ecological disasters in their wake. Prior to 1840 only a few dozen plants had been introduced; by 1930 there were more than a thousand. I have not mentioned cats because I love them, but honesty compels me to add that the Stephens Island wren was endemic to the island until 1894, when the government built a lighthouse there and installed a lighthouse keeper. He brought a cat, and this single cat eliminated the complete population of the wren in a single year. The introduction of cattle has still not received its full historical treatment anywhere as far as I know, though its effects have been devastating (in quality, if not quantity, along the lines of what is happening today in the Brazilian rain forest).

SOURCE: Plate 42 of the *New Zealand Historical Atlas*. A magnificent work, not to be missed, is H. Guthrie-Smith, *Tutira: The Story of a New Zealand Sheep Station*. Edinburgh and London: William Blackwood & Sons, 1953.

17. **1870–1970: The use of Maori in schools is actively discouraged.**

Although all Maori spoke their own language throughout the country, because of the gradual ascendancy of white culture, the Maori language was seen as an impediment to success. At first Maori was simply frowned upon, but eventually, starting from around 1900, Maori schoolchildren were punished if they used the language in school, and many Maori even began to abandon the language. It was thought (and in some so-called enlightened circles, is still thought) to be a dying language, with no future.

18. **1870: Wool is established as the mainstay of the New Zealand economy.**

Probably no society has ever existed without exploiting resources, and New Zealand is no exception. Native timber, kauri gum, and marine mammals were all destroyed by the Maori and the settlers alike, though the Maori at least recognized and respected limits. The existence of wool, of course, implies sheep (the first significant shipment of whom arrived as early as 1834), and sheep implies pasture. Since pasture does not exist without the clearing of land (by burning) and the planting of cultivated grass (imported from England!), the native New Zealand landscape had to be transformed or, better put, degraded to suit the world's taste for wool and, later (from 1880 on with the invention of refrigeration), meat. In

1879 there were around thirteen million sheep grazing on six thousand properties, and 27,777 tons of wool were exported to mills in Great Britain. The cost to the sheep, in suffering, has never been calculated.

SOURCE: For statistics, see plate 43 of the *New Zealand Historical Atlas*.

19. 1881: Invasion of Parihaka by the Crown.

In 1866 a new community was founded at Parihaka, at the foot of Mount Taranaki, based on the renunciation of war. The people wore white feathers in their hair as a symbol of their peaceful ways. Their leaders were Te Whiti o Rongomai and his brother-in-law Tohu Kakahi.

From 1869 Te Whiti began preaching the ultimate return of all confiscated Maori land (Parihaka was founded on confiscated land), using peaceful non-cooperation with the government. In 1879 they challenged the government, which claimed that the land was abandoned, and therefore government property, by plowing the land as soon as surveying began. Each day more and more men were arrested, but other tribes, especially from Waikato and Whanganui, sent more men to replace those arrested. Te Whiti regarded Parihaka as Israel (in the Pai Marire tradition) and stated: "No law of the Europeans shall govern the Maories." He wanted to replace the Treaty of Waitangi with a covenant that recognized the Maori as "owners of the soil." Links with other tribes grew by the day, and the government, in fear, reacted: On November 5, 1881, Parihaka was occupied by forces who expelled sixteen hun-

dred people, destroyed their homes, and arrested Te
Whiti, Tohu, and Titokowaru (another prophetic leader
who had fought a war in 1868–69). They were released
after two years, returning to Parihaka and beginning its
reconstruction. The community was born again as the
New Jerusalem in Canaan. They were rearrested, but continued to defy the government morally and physically
until the deaths of the two leaders in 1907.

SOURCE: Dick Scott, *Ask That Mountain: The Story of Parihaka*. Auckland: Reed,
1981. Hazel Riseborough, *Days of Darkness: Taranaki 1878–1884*. Wellington:
Allen & Unwin, 1989. Judith Binney's chapter, "Ancestral Voices: Maori Prophet
Leaders," in *The Oxford Illustrated History of New Zealand*. See especially the beau-
tiful book *Parihaka: The Art of Passive Resistance*, edited by Te Miringa Hohaia et al.
Wellington: Victoria University Press, 2001.

20. 1893: First country in the world to give women the vote.

This seems to have been a political move (to increase
votes in favor of temperance—as it turns out, a miscalcu-
lation) rather than a genuine gesture toward equality of
the sexes. Women were not eligible to be members of Parliament until 1919; the first woman to be elected was Eliz-
abeth McCombs, in 1933, and even that was to occupy the
seat vacated by her late husband. No woman held a cabinet post until Mabel Howard became minister of social
welfare in the Fraser Labour government in 1947. Even in
1960, women were insignificant in Parliament and local
politics. Today, while still underrepresented in politics,
women are serving as prime minister, chief justice, governor general, and head of the largest corporation (Tele-

com). Nonetheless, they are still poorer than men and more subject to domestic violence. Whether any country, let alone New Zealand, has or will ever have complete gender equality is questionable.

21. **1896: The Maori population is down to 40,000 (from an original 110,000).**

In 1881 the non-Maori population had soared to 470,000. Diseases brought by Western settlers were the main cause of the depopulation of Maori. Poverty, too, took its toll in poor health conditions. Alcohol often seemed the only emotional anesthetic, which only increased the suffering, and whole communities succumbed to despair, disease, and death. (Parihaka was an example of how this need not be the case; see item 19 above). Many so-called enlightened Western settlers were looking forward to the day there would be no Maori race, as if this would be a significant step forward for humankind as a whole.

22. **1898: Guaranteed old age pension.**

In response, Beatrice Webb, the well-known English socialist who, with her husband, Sydney, founded the London School of Economics, writes: "It is delightful to see a country with no millionaires and hardly any slums." Still *largely* true in 2004. William Pember Reeves, a political radical (too much so for the Liberal party when he was minister of labour 1892–96), a high commissioner in London, and the author of the first intelligent history of New Zealand, *The Long White Cloud*), said of the liberal reforms:

"They were the outcome of a belief that a young democratic country, still almost free from extremes of wealth and poverty, from class hatreds and fears and the barriers these create, supplies an unequalled field for safe and rational experiment in the hope of preventing and shutting out some of the worst social evils and miseries which afflict great nations alike in the old world and the new."

SOURCE: R. M. Chapman and Keith Sinclair, editors, *Studies of a Small Democracy*. Auckland: University of Auckland, 1963. David Hamer, *The New Zealand Liberals: The Years of Power, 1891–1912*. Auckland: Auckland University Press, 1988.

23. 1905: Beginnings of Sinophobia.

In Wellington in 1905, an elderly Chinese man was murdered by a European who wished to advertise his anti-Asiatic crusade. This anti-Chinese feeling has often been present in New Zealand society down to the present; I've been surprised to hear many comments about how the Chinese would turn Auckland into a den of iniquity. These are hardly distinct from views one hundred years ago that spoke of the danger from China in terms of women's virtue, drugs, perversions, gambling, and other vices. Perhaps for this very reason the Chinese tend to keep to themselves. Who can blame them? Xenophobia has played a role in New Zealand society despite the claim that there is no racial prejudice. Anti-Maori feeling is still very much alive, as are biases and prejudices against Indians, Pacific Islanders, and even certain European nations.

SOURCE: Ng B. Fong, *The Chinese in New Zealand: A Study in Assimilation*. Hong Kong: Hong Kong University Press, 1959.

24. 1907: Passage of the Tohunga Suppression Act.

A tohunga is a "chosen one," a combination priest, medicine man, shaman, and wise man. He is both respected and feared by Maori. Sir James Carroll, most senior Maori member of the House of Representatives at the time, with the backing of his protégé, Apirana Ngata, passed this law in the patronizing belief that superstition had no role in modern Maori society. The act was repealed in 1962. There is no doubt it did lasting damage to traditional Maori beliefs and practices since many of these resided with the tohunga, who then had to practice in secret if at all.

SOURCE: Paul Moon, *Tohunga: Hohepa Kereopa*. Auckland: David Ling Publishing, 2003.

25. 1907: Founding of the Plunket Society by Dr. Frederic Truby King.

King was a much-feared doctor with inane and destructive views: "Baby must NEVER sleep in bed with his mother." At the terrifying (throughout its entire history, but then I am biased against any psychiatric hospital) Seacliff Asylum in Dunedin, a woman whose sin in the eyes of Dr. King was that she was an "inveterate masturbator" had her ovaries and clitoris surgically removed at his insistence. Keith Sinclair, New Zealand's most distinguished historian, called him "arguably the most influential man in Pakeha society." His influence on women was enormous, especially through the Plunket Society, which he founded to propagate his views. Every child, even today, is visited by a Plunket nurse, though the views of its founder have long been relegated (I hope) to the rubbish bin of history where they belong.

SOURCE: James Belich, *Paradise Reforged: A History of the New Zealanders: From the 1880s to the Year 2000.* Auckland: Penguin, 2001. Also Linda Bryder, *Not Just Weighing Babies: Plunket in Auckland 1908–1998.* Auckland: Auckland University Press, 1998.

26. 1908: Beginnings of the trade union movement.

The Federation of Miners was founded in 1908, interested in social revolution. Real wages did not rise between 1900 and 1913 (except for miners), which contributed to an unprecedented discontent in the workforce. Strikes became common, the most famous being the Blackball Mine in 1908 where Pat Hickey (who had been a miner in Utah and a member of the "Wobblies," the much feared IWW, International Workers of the World) demanded that the miners' mealtime underground be increased from fifteen to thirty minutes. In 1913 employers locked out workers from the Wellington wharves. A national strike was called, but there was not enough national support and the strike collapsed. New Zealand politics was to remain polarized for a generation, and the labor movement was not to come to power until 1935, when everyone seemed in agreement that the goal was to "improve capitalism, not abolish it."

SOURCE: Michael King, *The Penguin History of New Zealand.*

27. 1935: World's first welfare state.

In November 1935 the Labour party came to power for the first time in New Zealand history. Society was ready for change and the party delivered, aided by the articulate and fiery John A. Lee (who hated the prime minister, Joseph Savage, who disliked him as well). Old age pensions were restored and increased; a forty-hour working week was introduced, as well as a minimum wage that could support a married couple and three children; and perhaps most important, a state housing scheme was begun, to provide for every New Zealander "a home fit for a Cabinet minister," and the Reserve Bank was instructed to finance such homes with credit that would be interest-free. The general public was ecstatic with these important reforms, many of them only dreamed about in other societies around the world.

SOURCE: Michael King, *The Penguin History of New Zealand.*

28. 1938: Social Security Act and Family Benefit Assistance are enacted.

In 1938 Parliament passed the Social Security Act mandating free health care, an old age pension at sixty, and retirement at sixty-five. In 1946 every family was given one pound per week. Erik Olssen, a historian who currently holds the James Cook Fellowship from the Royal Society of New Zealand, has written that New Zealand was now "back on its true course as the most advanced and humane society in the world."

29. 1940–50: New Zealand is the world's most prosperous country.

Nonetheless, Peter Buck, the Maori ethnologist of international renown, left the country for the Bishop Museum in Honolulu and Yale University, and many other scholars of note left because of the insularity of New Zealand and to seek larger career possibilities, prompting Margaret Mead to say: "It is New Zealand's role to send out its bright young men and women to help run the rest of the world. And they go, not hating the country of their birth but loving it. From this . . . base they make their mark on the world." (Quoted in Michael King, *The Penguin History of New Zealand,* page 417.)

30. 1940: Herbert Guthrie-Smith writes his book of environmental history, *Tutira: The Story of a New Zealand Sheep Station.*

    Guthrie-Smith asks: "Am I absolutely happy about my substitution of domestic breeds of animals for native lizards and birds; my substitution of one flora for another; my contribution towards more quickly melting New Zealand through erosion in the Pacific. . . . Have I then for sixty years desecrated God's earth and dubbed it improvement?" Deep questions, still in need of answers.

31. 1951: Maori Women's Welfare League formed.

    Whina Cooper was the first president of this influential body of Maori women. They assessed education, health, child, and housing needs and were able to bring political pressure to have them addressed in government policy. Play centers, both rural and urban—still an important part of children's lives today—were a creation of the league.

    Source: Michael King, *Whina Cooper.* Auckland: Hodder and Stoughton, 1987.

32. 1951: Waterfront lockout.

The longest strike in New Zealand history, it lasted 151 days. In response to the strike, the government, led by the National party, prohibited any publicizing of the workers' case and levied penalties for anybody who assisted the families of striking workers, even by providing food! The armed forces were called in to work the wharves. Labour opposition, led by Walter Nash, took a cowardly stance, saying they were "not for the waterside workers, and we are not against them."

SOURCE: Michael King, *The Penguin History of New Zealand.*

33. 1953: Edmund Hillary reaches the summit of Mount Everest.

See chapter 7 on Sir Edmund.

34. 1959: A Maori doctor, Harry Bennett, is refused service in a bar in Auckland.

True, this incident indicates that racism was alive and well in New Zealand, but compared with racism in the United States and in Australia, it was relatively benign. It is inconceivable that a lynching could have taken place in New Zealand at the time, while it was commonplace in the United States for many years later.

35. 1960: Barry Crump and his brand of Kiwi matehood achieve wide popularity.

"Giving the wife a bit of a clip around the ear-hole" was a trademark in the life of Barry Crump (a trick he learned from his father). How could these novels (*A Good Keen Man*) possibly have sold a million copies in New Zealand and have made Barry Crump the country's most successful writer ever? Because they belong to a tradition going back to John Mulgan's *Man Alone* (or the later version by Frank Sargeson, *That Summer*), where men see themselves living without women, in the bush, off the land, killing pigs with knives in hand-to-tusk combat, culling deer, binge drinking, and being violent toward men and women alike (the misogyny in these books must be read to be believed), a fantasy that seems to have had particular resonance in both New Zealand and Australian male culture. Did any woman ever buy his books? Good riddance to an old legend.

SOURCE: Colin Hogg, *A Life in Loose Strides: The Story of Barry Crump*. Auckland: Hodder Moa Beckett Publishers, 2000.

SOURCE: Jock Phillips, *A Man's Country: The Image of the Pakeha Male—A History*. Auckland: Penguin, 1996 (rev. ed.).

36. 1960s: Start of immigration from Pacific Islands. Major urbanization of the Maori population.

Auckland is today the world's largest Polynesian city. Tongans, Samoans, Niueans, and other Pacific Islanders came to Auckland because it was already a city heavily influenced by Maori culture, one especially close to them (according to Dr. Margaret Orbell, a scholar of classical Maori, Hawaiki itself is probably an island in the Samoan archipelago of Savai'i), but also, of course, for economic reasons. Of the two hundred thousand Pacific Islanders in New Zealand today, 70 percent live in Auckland. The Maori before the Second World War were predominantly rural (90 percent). In 1960 the Department of Maori Affairs encouraged rural families to shift from the "pipi beds" to urban areas. The problem was that they were sent to poorer, more dangerous neighborhoods, such as Otara or Otahuhu in South Auckland, where the Maori population is probably as high as 50 percent. Because traditional extended family life is most often disrupted in these moves, many of the younger men, longing for a feeling of belonging to a larger group (and feeling rejected by Pakeha society), gravitate toward the Maori gangs. I have been told that at least a third of all young Maori men cannot say what iwi ("tribe") they belong to.

SOURCE: Ranginui Walker, *Ka Whawhai Tonu Matou: Struggle Without End*. Auckland: Penguin, 1990.

37. 1972: Britain's entry into the Common Market.

This was a traumatic event for many New Zealanders, who still referred to England as the "mother country" and were used to sending their exports to England almost exclusively. Geographic logic suggested all along that Asia (Japan and Korea in particular) and the Pacific (Australia of course, but also Malaysia and Indonesia) were the obvious markets for New Zealand, but this took some time to sink in, and there still lingers in some people a sense of betrayal by the United Kingdom.

38. 1975: The Waitangi Tribunal is established to consider Maori land claims.

The tribunal comprised a chairman (chief judge of the Maori Land Court) and two appointees, one a Maori, the other a Pakeha lawyer. Though lacking powers of enforcement, the tribunal had enormous influence on public attitudes and could thereby affect government decisions. In 1985 an amendment act was passed expanding the size of the tribunal to six appointees, four being Maori; more important, the jurisdiction was broadened to allow the investigation of claims dating back to the original signing in 1840. On the other hand, it followed a Canadian model, becoming more of a research tool than a means of action.

SOURCE: Alan Ward, *An Unsettled History: Treaty Claims in New Zealand Today.* Wellington: Bridget Williams Books, 1999.

39. 1976: Overstayer crisis.

These were infamous dawn raids by immigration officers hunting for overstayers (i.e., people who stayed beyond what was permitted by their visas), a fact remembered with loathing and resentment by Pacific Islanders even today.

40. 1975–: Maori renaissance: Maori occupation of Bastion Point in 1975 and the Maori Land March from Cape Reinga to Wellington in 1975.

Ranginui Walker provides the history behind this historic occupation. This valuable land in the heart of Auckland clearly belonged to the Ngati Whatua iwi, but the govern-

ment sought it by a series of machinations beginning in
1840 and culminating in 1951, when the rightful owners
were evicted and their houses, including a sacred meetinghouse, were knocked down and burned. In January
1977 the Orakei Maori Action Group led by Joe Hawke
(who had, as a child, seen his house there burned to the
ground) occupied the land at Bastion Point to prevent its
subdivision. The high court ruled on a compromise that
the protesters rejected. An injunction for their removal
was ordered, and Maori elders begged the protesters to
leave. They refused. Finally, after 506 days, on May 25,
1978, six hundred policemen cleared the point. In the
summer of 1974–75 Dame Whina Cooper led the Land
March from the far north, where she set off with fifty
marchers carrying a banner and a flag: NOT ONE MORE ACRE
OF MAORI LAND. They stopped in maraes (Maori meeting
places) all through the country and held discussions;
more and more people flocked to the march. As they approached both Auckland and finally, eight months after
setting off, Wellington, their ranks swelled to tens of
thousands of people. A Memorial of Rights was handed
to Prime Minister Bill Rowling on the steps of Parliament
in Wellington.

From the late 1960s, one can speak of a Maori renaissance: increased interest in the Maori language, especially
at the university level; literature (Patricia Grace, Witi Ihimaera, Keri Hulme, and many others); film (*Once Were
Warriors*, but even more important, the startling interna-

tional success of *Whale Rider*); and art (as in the 1984 *Te Maori* exhibition that toured the United States).

SOURCE: Ranginui Walker, *Ka Whawhai Tonu Matou: Struggle Without End*. Auckland: Penguin, 1990.

41. 1981: Kohanga reos established.

When research in the 1970s showed that the Maori language was dying out, the Department of Maori Affairs decided to establish "language nests" (kohanga reos) where preschool children could be immersed in a Maori-speaking environment. The aim was to make all Maori children bilingual by the time they were five (and went to primary school). In 1994 there were 809 such schools around the country (where, by the way, Pakeha children are welcomed with open arms—as I know from visiting one). The mothers, too, became interested in learning more of their traditional language. A political element was added when a kohanga reo conference was convened at Turangawaewae Marae in 1984, and one thousand people attended.

42. 1981: Springbok Tour protests.

Discontent had been brewing for many years. In 1960 the All Blacks rugby team went to South Africa, but in deference to apartheid sentiments on the part of the host country, the team did not include any Maori players. A prominent historian, W. H. Oliver, said in his *The Story of New Zealand* (published in 1960): "Though many Maoris have achieved eminence in New Zealand's national preoccupation, Rugby football, Maoris do not travel in teams that tour South Africa. In this we may see the demands of sport taking precedence over the demands of racial harmony." In 1973 the Labour government under August Kirk compelled the New Zealand Rugby Football Union to call off a tour of New Zealand by the South African Springboks. This angered a large segment of the electorate. Under the National party, in 1976 the All Blacks rugby team toured South Africa amid protests by thousands of New Zealanders and worldwide pressure to adhere to a world boycott of the racist country. Finally in 1981 the South African Springboks toured New Zealand. The protest was immense, led by the Citizens Association for Racial Equality (CARE) and Halt All Racist Tours (HART), both of which still exist and which are now concerned with racism at home. There was violence and disorder in New Zealand that had not been seen for fifty years. Police in full riot gear appeared in the streets of the major cities, a fact shocking to most New Zealanders.

43. 1984: Cervical cancer scandal.

Sandra Coney, a leading feminist writer, and Phillida Bunkle published an article in the Auckland weekly *Metro* about a doctor who had been seeing women whose cervical smears indicated that they had cancer. The doctor then did nothing about it, to see if the results of inaction were any worse than those of aggressive therapy (with surgery, radiation, and chemotherapy). He did not tell the women either about the results of their smears or about his "research" project. The brilliant article (followed by a book) led to the longest Royal Inquiry in New Zealand's history and changed the face of medicine in this country. It is a tribute to the tenacity of lay women (not doctors) who refused to buckle under threats or intimidation and demanded answers to questions that involved the health and well-being of a huge number of women.

SOURCE: Sandra Coney, *The Unfortunate Experiment: The Full Story Behind the Inquiry into Cervical Cancer Treatment.* Auckland: Penguin, 1988.

44. 1984: Rogernomics.

This term refers to the economic policies of Finance Minister Roger Douglas, an accountant who believed in devolving or selling as much of New Zealand's inherited business as possible. Agriculture and consumer subsidies were phased out; the financial market was deregulated; the New Zealand dollar was floated for the first time; controls on foreign exchange were removed; the tax rate was reduced from 65 to 33 percent. Even his own colleagues did not realize what was happening until it was too late to act, and small communities lost their post office or forestry jobs. The prime minister, David Lange, hugely popular, was aghast at what he had unleashed, and finally resigned when the cabinet backed Douglas.

SOURCE: Brian Easton, editor, *The Making of Rogernomics.* Auckland: Auckland University Press, 1989.

45. 1985: *Rainbow Warrior* sunk.

The bombing (and total destruction) of the *Rainbow Warrior,* flagship of the environmental group Greenpeace, and the subsequent drowning of Fernando Pereira, one of its crew, was the first act of international terrorism in New Zealand waters. This led to the biggest police operation in New Zealand history and the jailing of two French agents. The French security service had bombed the ship to prevent its much-publicized voyage to Mururoa Atoll, where Greenpeace planned to disrupt French nuclear testing. The French government, and in particular François Mitterand, pretended to be shocked, horrified, and completely mystified by the "criminal attack which no excuse can justify." New Zealand sentenced both men to ten years' imprisonment on charges of manslaughter. The French minister of defense resigned. The French prevailed upon New Zealand to release the men to serve their time on the French island of Mayotte in the Indian Ocean, whereupon they were soon released, met at the airport by the new minister of defense, and treated as national heroes. Relations between France and New Zealand have remained to this day somewhat cool, which speaks well for New Zealand.

SOURCE: Michael King, *Death of the* Rainbow Warrior. Auckland: Penguin, 1986. See also the excellent chapter 9 in David Lange's book mentioned in the next item, "Enter the *Rainbow Warrior*," which gives an insider account of how the French twisted their way out of their obligations.

46. 1986: The Oxford Debate with David Lange.

David Lange, New Zealand Labour party prime minister, was asked to argue "nuclear weapons are morally indefensible" at a debate at the Oxford Union. His official advisers were appalled, thinking (correctly) that he would offend both the United States and Prime Minister Margaret Thatcher's government. His opponent? None other than Jerry Falwell, the evangelist from Lynchburg, Virginia, and founder of the Moral Majority. In the debate, Lange said, "I got the warmest response when I referred to American efforts to make an example of New Zealand. We were being told by the United States that we could not decide for ourselves how to defend ourselves, but had to let others decide that for us. That, I said, was exactly the totalitarianism we were fighting against. The audience roared." Lange won the debate and returned to New Zealand a national hero.

SOURCE: David Lange, *Nuclear Free: The New Zealand Way.* Auckland: Penguin, 1990.

47. 1987: Maori Language Act declares Maori an official language of New Zealand. Establishment of the Maori Language Commission.

48. 1987: New Zealand becomes a nuclear-free zone. David Lange, the prime minister under whose stewardship this happened, explains the essence very well at the end of his book *Nuclear Free:* "Given its [U.S.] strategy and enormous investment it could brook no dissent in the ranks. New Zealand's duty was to be uncomplainingly swept up in exactly the kind of international totalitarianism we were supposed to be ready to defend ourselves against. The rigour of this collective discipline was so important that the gross violation of New Zealand's sover-

eignty by France when it bombed the *Rainbow Warrior* and killed a man to avoid international publicity over its nuclear-testing programme went uncondemned and unremarked by the leaders of the Free World.... The exclusion of nuclear weapons from New Zealand was a small step to take in the global context, but unless a lot of small steps are taken we will always be in thrall to nuclear weapons." Bravo David Lange!

49. 1990: Ruthanasia.
   When the National government took office at the end of 1990 under Jim Bolger, the new finance minister, Ruth Richardson, was even more ruthless than her predecessor. Welfare was significantly reduced, and Housing New Zealand tenants, the very poor for whom these homes were initially built so they would not become homeless, were charged market rentals.

50. 2003: Maoris represent 15 percent of the population, and non-native-born New Zealanders will soon constitute almost half of the population.

For Further Reading
For those interested in further reading, I have tried to give just one reference per item, but I compiled the list after extensive reading. My main sources have been:

- James Belich, *Making Peoples: A History of the New Zealanders: From Polynesian Settlement to the End of the Nineteenth Cen-*

tury. Auckland: Penguin, 1996. *Paradise Reforged: A History of the New Zealanders: From the 1880s to the Year 2000.* Auckland: Penguin, 2001. Considered New Zealand's leading historian, Belich's books are essential reading, giving one intelligent author's views on most of the major issues of New Zealand history.

- Bob Brockie, editor, *The Penguin Eyewitness History of New Zealand: Dramatic First-Hand Accounts from New Zealand's History.* Auckland: Penguin, 2002.

- Tom Brooking and Paul Enright, *Milestones: Turning Points in New Zealand History.* 2nd ed. Palmerston North: Dunmore Press, 1999. A useful, simple guide, concise but with an intelligent viewpoint.

- Michael King, *The Penguin History of New Zealand.* Auckland: Penguin, 2003. Readable, literate, and fair; my only criticism of this book is that the quotations are not identified.

- Geoff Park, *Nga Uruora The Groves of Life: Ecology and History in a New Zealand Landscape.* Wellington: Victoria University Press, 1995. A haunting, evocative history, with superb color photographs by Craig Potton, that has become a classic for good reasons.

- Eric Pawson and Tom Brooking, editors, *Environmental Histories of New Zealand.* Melbourne: Oxford University

Press, 2002. Excellent collection of essays; essential reading.

- Geoffrey W. Rice, editor, *The Oxford History of New Zealand.* 2nd ed. Auckland: Oxford University Press, 1992. Each of the twenty-two chapters is written by a different historian, and they are uniformly good. (The first edition, considered the standard reference, was edited by W. H. Oliver and B. R. Williams in 1981.)

- Keith Sinclair, *The Oxford Illustrated History of New Zealand.* 2nd ed. Auckland: Oxford University Press, 1996 (1st ed., 1990). Each of the fifteen chapters is written by a different historian. More accessible than the previous volume, it is an equally valuable resource.

- Ranginui Walker, *Nga Tau Tohetohe: Years of Anger.* Auckland: Penguin, 1987. A "radical" (in the best sense of the word) Maori perspective by a well-respected scholar. I learned much from reading this book.

chapter 5

Mad About the Trees, Not to Mention the Birds

Tim Flannery, director of the South Australian Museum in Adelaide, on the glorious birds that once sang in Aotearoa:

I would gladly remain ignorant of the joy of the *Haka,* or even the heart-stopping beauty of dame Kiri Te Kanawa singing *Songs of the Auvergne,* for the privilege of waking to a symphony of "the most tuneable silver sound imaginable." Aotearoa's multitudes of birds performed that symphony each dawn for over 60 million years. It was a glorious riot of sound with its own special meaning, for it was a confirmation of the health of a wondrous and unique ecosystem. To my great regret, I arrived in New Zealand in the late twentieth century only to find most of the orchestra seats empty. Walking through the ancient forest, whose still-living trees were once browsed by moa, I heard nothing but the whisper of leaves blowing in the wind. It was like the rustle of the last curtain fall on an orchestra that will be no more.

Is there something special about New Zealand because of the fact that it was one of the last places on earth to be discovered then settled by humans? Humans inhabited every single continent as recently as ten thousand years ago. New Zealand alone remained uninhabited. It had been that way for some 680 million years. In geological time, humans arrived just a few seconds ago. No other large island was so isolated for so long as New Zealand. For reasons that remain mysterious, there were virtually no mammals on New Zealand until they were introduced in the nineteenth century. Plants and birds and insects evolved in their own strange ways, not needing to heed human ways at all.

Unquestionably the greatest disturbance of all was created by human habitation; our arrival is the geological equivalent of a meteor falling from outer space—with equally devastating effects. "Human" here is not restricted to Europeans. By 1770, when Captain Cook arrived in New Zealand, half the bird species on the island were already extinct. There is something truly awe inspiring about listening to native bellbirds or tui singing a song they sang millions of years ago when there were no humans to hear their melodious sounds. Similarly, walking in kauri forests containing individual trees thousands of years old is not the same thing as walking down a quiet country lane. It is something for which words like *humbling* or even a religious term such as *tremendum* were created.

It did not always appear this way to the first settlers, whether Maori or Europeans. On the contrary, their feelings were probably more akin to the uncanny than to religious awe. The land was not familiar; the birds, the trees, the animals (or lack of animals) struck them as something to be regretted, not celebrated. The Maori wanted to re-create the tropical South Sea island they came from, probably one of the Society Islands; the English wanted to turn the islands into English countryside. They wanted hills filled with sheep, not with odd parrots or fern tree forests. By and large, the Maori did better with what they found, perhaps because the differences were not quite so stark and formidable. Yes, the moa and other birds were gone, and many of the trees, too, but the depradation was by no means total or irreversible. For that to happen, Europeans had to come in large numbers and to try to bend the land to their own limited and artificial usages.

I cannot deny that I find the country beautiful. But it may be that my sense of beauty has been constructed by what I already know. Every once in a while there is a glimmer of a different kind of beauty, of an original beauty, hints of what the country was like before a single human had set foot here. Yes, that is what I would like to know, to enjoy, but of course it is the ultimate paradox: By definition I cannot experience New Zealand the way it was before humans arrived because I am a human and I have arrived. How could I see it without being here? How could I not affect what I see if my very presence is proof that irreversible changes have already set in? And still we long for that time before humans. What a strangely perverted species we are!

Why do I long to see a moa, the last of whose kind was killed before any European had arrived in New Zealand? What is the thrill I can imagine of seeing this long-gone gentle giant of a bird? Is it just because there is the promise of a kind of Garden of Eden, a place where there is so little predation that birds have not needed flight feathers and have evolved to feel no fear? Is this longing for the peaceable kingdom inborn into all humans? Do we have some dim recollection of a time when we neither feared, nor were feared, or is that merely my own personal fantasy, unsupported by any facts about human evolution?

And yet if there exists any country that might satisfy this ancient craving to be a mere spectator, an insignificant player in nature, New Zealand is that place, and perhaps that explains some of its formidable attraction.

But I, too, remain a person with loyalties to my own human version of imprinting. I, too, can resonate to seeing a pig on a beach. In fact, that is how I came to be in New Zealand. We were just passing through. A friend in Australia knew I was writing about the emotional world of farm animals, and suggested I look up Tony Watkins, a professor of town planning at the University of Auckland, who happened to live on a beach (Karaka Bay) with Piglet, a large domestic pig. The pig, we were told, enjoyed swimming in the ocean and was not averse to children riding on her back. Nothing natural about it, you might think, but I had to see it. Alas, Piglet was a source of friction among some of the neighbors and had long since retired to a vast macadamia nut orchard in Northland (where I was to visit her many times in the coming years), but I fell in love with the bay itself, her first home, and could not tear myself away. I saw hundreds of pictures of Piglet, though, and if walking along the beach followed by numerous children was not part of her natural behavior, it did not look like unnatural behavior, either. She seemed to enjoy it immensely, and the children were of course enchanted. Despite her weight, she did not seem to have much of a negative impact on her surroundings. Maybe she had learned to live more lightly on the earth than did her human keepers.

My cat was another story, and I soon learned why so many biologists in New Zealand regard cats as the ultimate enemy of the native fauna, and take great pride in ridding specific islands of all such introduced predators. For millions of years native birds and other animals (insects and lizards, for example) had adapted to an environment lacking in mammalian predators. They had not learned to sufficiently fear these new, introduced animals, and now are constantly taken (literally) by surprise at their treacherous predatory skills. They have learned to adapt to one niche, and are required to make a sudden readjustment for which there is simply not enough time to lay down any genetic predisposition. So they are massacred in large numbers. It is not right. The cats, on the other hand, have no say in the matter; it is hardly a question of choice. Cat instincts evolved in a completely different situation as well, and it is no fault of their own that they find themselves inhabiting a niche requiring almost no predatory instincts for successful hunting. It is no doubt as confusing to them as it is to their prey. Both are in the wrong place at the wrong time. And at whose feet must all the blame be laid? Ours, of course. The Maori probably did not know what depredations would be unleashed by the rats brought along on the canoes, any more than the settlers knew what their cats and dogs would do to their environment. We cannot know that they would care even if they did know. Thinking of the long-term consequences in an altruistic fashion is probably a fairly recent acquisition by a still very limited number of members of our species.

This is one of the reasons why I find it hard to enjoy the bucolic scene of sheep grazing peacefully on a hillside in the New Zealand countryside. I immediately calculate the number of native trees that had to be removed for the sheep to be there in the first place. They seem out of place to me. They *are* out of place. Moreover, I know that the life they lead is not quite as peaceful as it seems to us from the outside (see my *The Pig Who Sang to the Moon: The Emotional World of Farm Animals*), and that the appearance of a blissful and harmless slow passage into old age is simply an illusion. Forty-three million sheep in a country of four million people just means that there is less native land, and more animal suffering. It is not the pretty picture it appears to many to be. This is why, in what follows, I try to take as much pleasure as possible in the native animals, primarily birds, and native trees, and native plants.

I never used to understand the American obsession with bird-watching. What difference could it possibly make that *you* happened to have seen a red-crested grebe? This was before I began to read more widely in the ornithological literature. Soon, while I did not see the point of merely *sighting* a bird, I could certainly understand why great biologists, such as Alexander F. Skutch (now nearing one hundred!), could devote their lives to the study of bird behavior. My lack of interest was a product of my ignorance. Even the simple joy of seeing a bird for the first time became more apparent to me the minute I actually began to notice the birds around me. That happened here in New Zealand.

The one bird I have failed to see, hard as I try, is the national bird of New Zealand, the kiwi. Actually, that is not surprising. Outside a zoo, few people have ever seen a kiwi. They are rare, they are nocturnal, and they are shy. They are also fascinating: The males make great dads; probably because the female is so exhausted by producing an egg almost half her body weight, the male takes full responsibility for brooding the single egg, for almost three months! Nobody knows just how many kiwis are left, but not many, perhaps fifty or sixty thousand. Think of it: About seven hundred years ago, before any humans had arrive in New Zealand, there were up to twelve million kiwis at any given time in the forests. They had no enemies before we arrived, the consummate hunter, the ultimate predator.

New Zealand as a whole, among the most isolated of the world's landmasses, is a bit like the Galapagos Islands, a place where many animals, and birds in particular, had never learned to fear predators because they had so few. Around 120 million years ago the Tasman Sea made its first appearance, and Gondwanaland, a composite continent made up of South America, Africa, Antarctica, India, and Australia, began to separate. Over the next hundred million years New Zealand, now separated from other lands by vast distances, began to develop a unique fauna and flora. Tim Flannery says, "Until 800 years ago New Zealand had the most extraordinary, indeed unbelievable, assemblage of birds. Nothing like it was found anywhere else on earth." For reasons that are not entirely clear, almost no mammals were left on the islands known as New Zealand. Without dangerous mammals, the birds were in little danger from predators. As a consequence, they never really learned to be frightened, and many of them lost the ability to fly, if they ever had it.

This is especially true of the moa (*Dinornis giganetus*), a bird belonging to the same family as other large, flightless birds, such as the Australian emu, the cassowary, and the ostrich. The moa, however, was even larger than the biggest ostrich. With his neck outstretched, he could reach nine feet tall, and weigh as much as 550 pounds. There are people in New

Zealand who claim to see them today, but in fact the last moa died at least three hundred years ago. The Maori hunted them to extinction. The bird had no instinctual fear of humans, and simply approached the Maori, who slaughtered them in huge numbers. Tim Flannery recounts that at one butchering site alone, the Waitaki mouth in the Otago District, "it is estimated that between 30,000 and 90,000 moa were killed." That is at a single site! The Maori also used their giant eggs as water gourds, and burned forests on which these gentle giants depended. In just a few hundred years, millions of years of moa history were ended. By the time the Europeans arrived, there were no more moa for them to kill, which they certainly would have done straightaway.

While driving through the wonderful rain forest suburb of Titirangi, just half an hour from Auckland, we saw a road leading to Huia and found ourselves entering an enchanted landscape that reminded me powerfully of the windward side of Oahu. There were tall cliffs covered in green vegetation (and a few modern houses) coming right down to the turquoise waters of the bay. We were with friends from the area, and when I asked where the name *Huia* came from, I was told it referred to yet another bird no longer to be seen. The last authenticated sighting of a huia (*Heteralocha acutirostris*) was in 1907. New Zealand's best-known ornithologist, Sir Walter Buller, tells us, without meaning to, why: "While we were looking at and admiring this little picture of bird-life, a pair of Huias, without uttering a sound, appeared in a tree overhead, and as they were caressing each other with their beautiful bills, a charge of No. 6 brought both to the ground together." He is sad, but happy to have "two fine specimens." Traditionally, only Maori chiefs were allowed to wear the feathers of this beautiful bird, and that no doubt hastened their decline. A prominent ornithologist recorded that eleven Maori hunters killed 646 huia in a single month! At least thirty-five species of birds became extinct from the time Maori arrived in New Zealand until Captain Cook's first voyage here, and a further seven species have become extinct—including the New Zealand quail, the piopio or New Zealand thrush, and the laughing owl—since European settlement. A large number are also today considered highly endangered—not surprising when you consider the philosophy of Sir Walter Buller, the nineteenth-century ornithologist who lamented their passing into extinction even as he shot the bird.

The only way to survive human greed and fantasy is to be seen as useless. This could explain why the pukeko (*Porphyrio porphyrio melanotus*) is still very much with us in New Zealand. Known in Europe as the swamp hen, this colorful bird the size of a large chicken somehow managed to migrate from Australia in the last thousand years without being a very enthusiastic flier. (I see them daily here, but have yet to see one fly.) They have, though, been very cautious about humans. Or just very smart. One of the few birds to have a special alarm call for an aerial predator as opposed to a ground animal (such as the introduced stoat), they are communal-minded birds. Not only do males help raise chicks, but they also will help other males raise their chicks, something practically unknown in the bird world. Within a group, males and females mate freely, meaning that the father is never certain who his own chicks are, which could explain why he is so helpful; it could be his own chicks he is protecting and nourishing. In any event, it is a brilliant strategy for long-term survival, which every animal would do well to imitate! Evidently they taste very bad, which may also have ensured their survival. (The Maori joke is that to cook one you put it in the ground with hot stones for a month, then dig up and throw away the bird and eat the stones.) I see them in duck ponds here, getting on very well with all the other birds in the area, yet another good trait of this ideal citizen.

But if nobody will ever see a friendly moa again, we can have the delight of seeing an equally friendly tiny little bird known as the North Island fantail (*Rhipidura fulginosa placabilis*) or piwakawaka. Everyone here has had the same experience: You are walking along a path in native bush, when suddenly a small bird comes up to within inches of your face and does a little dance, spreading its tail (hence the name) and seeming to want to make your acquaintance. I have had these charming birds follow me for up to half an hour. I am convinced they do it because they like our company, but a more competent biologist friend tells me that they are only interested in eating the insects we flush by our footsteps. This it easily does by spreading its tail and stopping in midflight to change direction. Well, even if they don't follow me because they like me, I am still convinced they are grateful to me for my cooperation in their feeding. I have never heard of anybody hunting these delightful little birds, and maybe that is an extra reason for them to be friendly with us.

It is a pity, though, that the parrots of Australia are not here in any number. For sheer beauty, nothing can surpass parrots. New Zealand does have a few native species, but they are rare enough that you are unlikely to spot one. There is the raucous kaka (*Nestor meridionalis*), an endemic New Zealand forest parrot. Much sought after by Maori for the red feathers under their wings, there are probably less than ten thousand left in the whole of New Zealand. In 1997 Sir David Attenborough, saddened by their fate, launched a major conservation program aimed at eliminating introduced enemies in a limited area, such as rats, stoats, and possums. It is too early to tell if it will be successful.

There is the kakapo (*Strigops habroptilus*)—the Maori word for "night parrot"—a heavy parrot (seven pounds!), flightless and nocturnal (so that the giant eagle could not find it). It is one of the most endangered birds in the entire world. In 1997, after three chicks were successfully hatched, the population was a mere fifty-four. It is the cat of parrots, for it is almost entirely solitary, something rare in the parrot family. Charlie Doublas, an explorer from Scotland who wandered the west coast of the South Island from 1867 until 1916, wrote of how easy it was then to capture this slow-moving bird: "... They could be caught in the moonlight, by simply shaking the tree or bush until they tumbled on the ground, something like shaking down apples. I have seen as many as half a dozen kakapos shaken off one tutu bush this way."

The kea (*Nestor notabilis*), also known as the mountain parrot, is another story. The world's sole alpine parrot, it thrives only in the high country of the South Island. When we were visiting Mount Cook, we saw many of them and had firsthand experience of their renowned cheekiness. They seem to have no instinctive fear of humans and will steal anything with fat on it right out of your knapsack. The common story of "rogue" keas driving sheep over cliffs and feasting on their kidneys is apparently no more than a legend indulged in by disgruntled sheep farmers, but a documentary film caught them attacking sheep (probably, though, only sick or dying animals), and there is now some evidence that they did the same thing to the moa! Even though they are easy to see, there are probably no more than about two thousand of them in existence, which shows how unsecretive they are. Just why they are so confident is mysterious.

Why do we miss the sounds of the birds of our home country? Well, clearly because we are used to them. I get as much pleasure from hearing the morepork as any Kiwi, but—and here is an essential difference—for a Kiwi who has been away in England, say, for ten years, and returns, and hears his first morepork, the impact is enormous. It brings with it all the feelings and memories and experiences of what he has missed in England. It is like music unheard for years; when you do hear it, you are suddenly and powerfully (and sometimes painfully) reminded of all the feelings you had when you last heard that music. Birds, after all, are musicians. The sound of the morepork (*Ninox novaeseelandiae*) calling at night has a special haunting quality that impresses everyone who hears it. Although I have never seen one, I hear them every night here on the beach. To the Maori, the sound resembled "ru ru"—hence the Maori name for the bird is ruru. To Westerners, however, the cry sounded like "more pork." It is a nocturnal owl, the only native owl in New Zealand. (In fact, there is one other, the little owl, introduced from Germany.) Why the sound should be associated with nostalgic sadness, I do not know, but that seems to be the experience of many people. A point they were formerly reluctant to concede, ornithologists are now prepared to admit that birds sing from sheer joy, as well as for territorial reasons (hence it is mostly male birds who sing, though not exclusively). But I think ornithologists would draw the line at saying that a bird sings out of sadness. I think we are safe to conjecture that the sadness humans hear in the morepork's call is our interpretation, a genuine case of anthropomorphism—something I am rarely willing to concede!

By the way, if you are visiting Auckland, do not miss the opportunity to take the ferry to the island of Tiritiri Matangi, a bird refuge less than an hour away from the city by boat. You will have lunch on a lush lawn and, if you are lucky, you will be visited by the rarest of all New Zealand birds, the takahe (*Porphyrio mantelli*). In fact, you will *definitely* be visited and bothered by this bird, and his brothers and sisters as well. There may be only a few dozen on the island, but they like to hang out where there are picnics and have no fear whatsoever of you. They resemble a much fatter pukeko, and are in fact closely related (as the Latin name indicates). The remarkable thing about these birds is that by the end of the nineteenth century they were believed to be extinct in New Zealand. A doctor from Invercargill, Geoffrey Orbell, in the far south of the South Island, was sure they were still extant, when one glorious day in 1948 he found a pair in Fiordland in the Murchison Mountains. It turned out that there were probably two to three hundred of them there. A few were introduced to Tiritiri, and they seem to be doing very well. The young, however, must be taught, by aversion therapy, to be afraid of stoats, their mortal enemy. An ornithologist shows the takahe chicks a puppet show in which a stuffed stoat beats up a takahe glove puppet. A week later, they are shown the stuffed stoat, and immediately hide!

Because they are introduced species—even though some of them are self-introduced—I have not mentioned here many birds whom I like to observe, and who give me great pleasure; for example, the colorful kingfishers from Australia (related to the marvelous kookaburra, the laughing bird). (Can I say that I get more pleasure from watching the native oystercatchers, who are plentiful along my beach? Well, maybe I can, just because I have learned that they are more attentive parents than practically any other bird. I notice that the seagulls are constantly bothered by their young, who pester them incessantly for food, in vain. But the oystercatcher seems to like feeding her youngster! By the way, talk about tool use: The reason these birds got their name is because they are so adept at opening oysters, which they often do by hammering them against rocks, an art it can take years to perfect and must be learned from their loving parents.)

Some introduced bird species are irresistible, such as the California quail, running with their black plumes above their head, followed by little black quail-dots, their babies. I also find Canada geese wonderful birds to observe, but I understand they are considered a pest. Still, *pest* is one of those words whose use needs justification. Merely because the Canada goose fouls pastures in Canterbury, New Zealand, does not make it, in my eyes, worth destroying. I have a more difficult time with the Australian magpie and the Asian mynah bird. They are fun to watch, but I know that the mynah, in any event, attacks other native birds and will destroy their eggs and chicks. Moreover, when we think about it, we can understand that the native birds were designed to live in native forests. When humans came along and turned those forests into pastures or cities, these same birds were bound to be confused. The introduced species, on the other hand, have an advantage and thrive on the changes. It is a fact that no endemic birds have increased since human settlement, except for the paradise shelduck (because they mate for life?). I love watching the many species of seagulls that congregate on our beach all day long, and when I think about some of their feats of migration, I feel humbled. The arctic tern (*Sterna paradisaea*), for example, goes to and from the poles, and since they live for thirty years, an individual bird can travel six hundred thousand miles! The Pacific golden plover regularly travels from New Zealand to

Alaska. Are these birds citizens of Alaska or New Zealand? How much I love the fact that nobody asks them for a passport. How long will it take until we are so free?

If I have not spoken here about penguins, it is only because I have failed to see any since I have been in New Zealand. This despite the fact that no other country has as many penguin species as New Zealand: thirteen of the world's eighteen. The blue penguin (korara, also called, in Australia, the fairy penguin) is the smallest of all penguins, and is often seen near populated areas such as Wellington and Oamaru (where we arrived too early to see them returning from the sea—evidently a wonderful sight). They are so noisy that people who have them nesting in their basements complain they cannot sleep at night!

*M*ost people like birds because of the songs they sing. If you fall into that category, you will be happy in New Zealand. Joseph Banks, the naturalist on James Cook's first expedition (and the founder of Kew Gardens in London), wrote, famously, of his first hearing of the native birds: "This morning I was awakd by the singing of the birds ashore. . . . [Their] voices were certainly the most melodious wild musick I have ever heard, almost imitating small bells but with the most tuneable silver sound imaginable."

I have heard few birds more melodious than the tui (*Prosthemadera novaeseelandiae*), also known as the parson bird because of a small tuft of white feathers around the black neck. Ornithologists from the Northern Hemisphere, where only male birds sing, were astonished to hear the glorious sounds of the female tui, who sings even when she is on her nest. They are remarkable mimics, and you will often hear what you think is a cat or a morepork, only to spot this delightful singer sitting in your karaka tree singing her heart out as a feline or an owl. The sound of this bird is not always easy to distinguish from the bellbird (*Anthornis melanura*), or korimako, who can also imitate cats and moreporks. Captain James Cook, when he first heard a bellbird in New Zealand, wrote in his journals: "This wild melody was infinitely superior to any that we had ever heard of the same kind; it seemed to be like small bells most exquisitely tuned."

I remember the first time I saw a kereru (also called a kukupa in Maori), or native wood pigeon. I heard a great swooshing of wings, as of a very large bird, and then saw what looked like a combination of an ordinary rock pigeon—the kind we see in our cities and give so little thought to—and a dazzlingly colored parrot. Taking to the air from the middle of the bush, it was a wonderful sight, but I realized it would be fairly rare. Their numbers are decreasing everywhere. The Maori have traditionally eaten them, yet they have been officially fully protected since 1921 (it is not at all certain they can survive), which poses an insoluble conflict between the two cultures. In some areas, such as Whangarei, just north of Auckland, it turns out the kereru die by the time they are three, long before they are able to reproduce. Though descended from an ancestral fruit pigeon from New Caledonia, the kereru has been in New Zealand for several million years, and has evolved into a quite distinct species. It is now the only bird who can swallow and spread large seeds throughout native forests. As Gerard Hutching, the editor of *Forest and Bird* in New Zealand, puts it: "Kereru eat the fruits of at least seventy species of plants and have an average feeding territory of twenty-five square kilometers, making them the most important seed-dispersing birds in New Zealand forests ... the kereru has become a pivotal species for the continued health of the forest, making its preservation of far-reaching importance."

You don't normally think of orcas (*Orcinus orca*) as belonging to any particular place, though I suppose people in the state of Washington will not agree, nor will our neighbors here in Karaka Bay, for we often see them swimming languidly up the bay between our beach and the nearest island, just a mile or so offshore. Nobody is certain how many live around the New Zealand coast (and *live* is used loosely here, since unlike us, orcas do not have an address), but there are no more than two hundred. They are incredibly long-lived, possibly to eighty years old, and only become sexually mature by the age of twelve to fifteen, much like humans. Just why it should be such a thrill to see them swimming past our house, I am not sure, but it certainly is, and neighbors tell neighbors and we all congregate on the beach to watch, struck by something we cannot name.

What counts as "interesting"? Every time I think I have reached my limit, I realize that that limit needs revision. Partly it is a function of simple knowledge: The more we know about anything, the more interesting it becomes, the more worthy of our attention and protection. Who would dare proclaim Darwin's fascination with barnacles idle curiosity? In my case, my newfound interest in volcanoes is more aesthetic, I concede, than scientific. I know little about geology, but I love the fact that New Zealand is a major center of volcanic activity. Possibly the world's largest eruption in the last million years occurred right here, from Lake Taupo, just a few hours' drive from Auckland. That was probably a long time ago, but much more recently, in fact in 181 CE, Chinese astronomers noted atmospheric disturbances from an enormous explosion from the same lake. For some reason, I have taken particular pleasure in walking to the top of all the accessible volcano craters in Auckland, some sixteen of them. Their sacred character (especially to the Maori) is not always respected, and it is sad to see that the volcano in the suburb of Three Kings, is rapidly disappearing to the greed of an ugly quarry. To think that this volcano lasted for thousands, perhaps millions of years, only to be destroyed to make building material.

*J*ust as I am slowly beginning to see the attraction in birdwatching, or at least in listening to, observing, and thinking about birds and their lives, I am also beginning to awaken to the marvels of trees. This has taken me longer than it has taken others. I never doubted, of course, that trees were living beings, but I can remember thinking that if I were to write a book called *The Emotional Lives of Trees* probably nobody would be interested in reading it (finding the material to write it is another matter altogether), whereas now I realize that when somebody finally *does* write such a book (and the day will inevitably come) it will be an enormous bestseller. If there was one part of Tolkien's *Lord of the Rings* that I found irresistible, it was when the trees came to life and took part in the battle to save Middle Earth. I attribute my conversion, however, to living in New Zealand, that is, in close proximity to remarkable trees. There is already a book, and a fine one, titled *Meetings with Remarkable Trees;* otherwise it would be my ambition to write such a book.

You have to wonder whether trees have feelings, or wills, or consciousness—all words that describe states humans find useful and that are now, long overdue, being gingerly used for other animals, mainly mammals, but also, even more gingerly by scientists, for birds. But for trees and plants? True, there was a sensational book in 1973, *The Secret Life of Plants,* by Peter Tompkins and Christopher Bird, about how talking to plants makes them happy and healthy, but Tompkins went on to espouse increasingly dotty ideas (about Rudolph Steiner and theosophy, garden spirits and Wilhelm Reich all mixed in with loopy conspiracy theories), and serious scientists stayed away. Still, could there not be forms of consciousness and realms of feeling that are not recognizable to us, but nonetheless real to trees?

I am a great fan of the much-detested term *political correctness.* I always fail to see why intellectuals, especially, feel that if something is politically correct they must oppose it or sneer at the idea behind it. After all, it only means that somebody has thought about the political implications of something, and persuaded people that there is a hidden politics, which ought to be attended to. If it is politically correct to use a certain term, that is only because we are used to denigrating whole groups of people in our language without paying the slightest attention to how they might feel about our use of such words. Surely the target group knows in greater depth how words affect them?

Perhaps, though, I have carried this too far when it comes to plants. Leila and I wanted to use only "native" plants in our garden, avoiding exotic, introduced species, even if we find them beautiful to look at. Yesterday on the Coromandel Peninsula, that wonderful area two hours from Auckland, I was walking by a house with two magnificent, giant trees in the front yard. I asked the woman what kind of trees they were, and she told me they were magnolia trees, planted there 150 years ago by the man who discovered gold in Coromandel. He had brought them back from California! Would I not want such trees there? They took my breath away. We really wanted a tropical garden in our front yard, but planted only native trees, whereas all our neighbors have groves of introduced banana trees, and lovely papaya trees. (Well, actually we do have a few.)

I have trouble, still, in deciding what is a weed and what is a plant. Is this not a human distinction? What we like is by definition not a weed. Our roof is covered in various grasses and some of my neighbors think I should "weed" it more, but I cannot determine what is a weed and what is a grass. My only criterion is what I like to look at. I suppose if I knew that one species was choking another, was more aggressive, I might be aggressive in my turn. I like a wild look, though. I also like the feel of a tropical island. Parts of the North Island where I live remind me more of Hawaii than of Northern California. After all, there are now lots of papaya trees growing in the hills behind our beach. Banana trees are also everywhere here, whole stands of them. And where in California do you have mangrove forests at the edge of the ocean? When we drive north, to the Hokianga, we see literally thousands of acres of mangrove forest along the shore. I love them, because I know that they are among the most fertile ecosystems in the world (producing four times as much plant matter as the very best pasture does), and are home to hundreds of animal species that would not survive without their protection. Many people are unaware of how important mangroves are to prevent coastal erosion and as a nursery for fish, and they use them as dumping grounds. That is changing, however, and I am delighted to see the many boardwalks that the Department of Conservation (DOC) has erected in mangrove swamps for walking and enjoying the bird life that is so rich in these areas.

It is no use pretending that New Zealand is completely free from a special form of xenophobia that dislikes not only foreign *people* but foreign *anything*. Every country, and every people in history, has had some form of this and to some degree. Only gradually is this special form of narrow-mindedness losing its grip on humanity. Fortunately, we don't really supply dogs and cats and trees and birds with nationality, do we? I think the key concept may be one of displacement. We do not want to displace what is already there, but could we not give equal value to what has just come? If we think of displacement as in water, we realize that one does not exclude the other. You just add room. What has been here a while deserves our respect, and that which has "just arrived" can bring new ideas and information. Ideally, there is a respect for what is already there, and a special welcome of what or who is coming in.

Alas, it has never worked that way in reality. The concept of "native"—as in a native plant, a native animal, and especially a native person—has always been politically loaded, and usually for good reason. Even if, as recent research suggests, the Maori came to New Zealand only eight hundred years ago, that is still a *long* time earlier than the first settlers from Europe. It *is* their land. As a recent arrival, I am conscious of the resonance of the word *recent* and wonder, *How old is recent?* In my defense, I like to think that I give equal weight to my eighty-five-year-old mother and our twenty-two-month-old toddler. Each has a right to be here. If we get too strict, we are not that far off the German botanists who in 1942 wanted to "cleanse the German landscape of unharmonious foreign substance"— so only native plants along the *autobahn, bitte.* They were explicit—a native plant along the Reich's motor highways was like the Aryan purification of people. This is why S. J. Gould warned against the notion that "my 'native' is best, and yours fit only for extirpation."

We can see something of this in the almost passionate New

Zealand hatred of the Tasmanian possum (or opossum, depending on where you are from), *Trichosurus vulpecula*. True, there are more than sixty million, and equally true that each night these vegetarians gobble up twenty thousand tons of vegetation. Moreover, in their native Australia the eucalyptus trees have a natural toxin lacking here in New Zealand, and there are few natural predators to eat them, so the damage they cause to native forests—and by extension to the native bird population, which depends on these forests—is extensive. More than fifty million dollars are spent each year in killing and researching ways to murder possums. A good Kiwi is supposed to buy possum fur products, whereas the rest of the world has more or less shunned it. I don't know the solution (sterilization seems to me promising), but I do know that we have not found it, and that finding the easy path to possum genocide is not the ideal way to solve a human-caused problem.

But back to trees. True, some of the non-native trees displace native ones. What if we were not to think this way, though, and on the contrary saw trees as all native in some sense—that is, they deserve to stay where they are, to have the right not to be cut down, removed, burned, destroyed, or maimed, if only out of respect for the fact that they have made it this far? It is hard to see the damage that an "introduced" tree can do. Botanists say they take over—the eucalyptus, for example—but I can't see irreparable damage, and I say let a million plants grow! Not everything "introduced" is automatically bad. (We may have been too purist about wanting only native plants in our garden.) Everything had to come from somewhere at some point, including, of course, most notoriously, *us!* Humans are the ultimate introduced species, and we have not been terribly beneficial wherever we go, either. I am not always sure what is introduced and what is not and how one can tell. There are eighteen hundred species of praying mantises in the world, and New Zealand only has one, the *Orthodera ministralis*, who, gratefully, does not decapitate her mate while copulating. I love watching them climb over my green plants in the garden. At certain times of the year they are everywhere, and I find them fascinating. I have refrained from asking more knowledgeable friends if the praying mantis is introduced or native, because I do not want to spoil my pleasure.

When I had my first cold in New Zealand, I was advised by neighbors to take lots of "manuka" honey. This is honey produced from the flower of the native manuka plant, a key pollen plant for honeybees (and green geckos!, not to mention kiwis). Honeybees, however, are not native to New Zealand. And the native bee that takes the pollen of the manuka does not make honey. So if people want to eat honey, they must take it from non-native bees, getting it from a native plant. It gets complicated. Of course you could solve the dilemma by saying that you will not rob bees of their own product (a respectable position—one taken, for example, by vegans), but then what do you do for your cold? The curative powers of this remarkable plant have been long known. Captain Cook already dubbed it the "tea tree," because he brewed tea from its leaves, something he no doubt learned from the Maori, who use different parts of it (such as chewing the shoots to cure dysentery) for curing all kinds of ailments—sore throat, back pain, eye problems. The leaves are pungent, and so strong is the brew that few come back for a second cup! Scientists in New Zealand are hard at work at present to find the major antibacterial component of the aromatic acids in the honey. Of course the fact that it is a folk remedy does not mean it does not work. There are whole forests of manuka (up to thirty-five feet tall), the most common and best known of all New Zealand plants, which sometimes looks more like a tree than a simple plant (and sometimes not; it can just creep along the ground in some environments), growing throughout the whole of New Zealand. You know you are in such a forest when you are suddenly overwhelmed with a sweet smell (found in the flowers, the seeds, the leaves, and even the young shoots) and then you notice the white (sometimes pink) flowers on the tree from September until February. From a distance you could think that snow had fallen, so thick are these beautiful flowers. Beneath its protection, the ground is sometimes covered with orchids. I still find it difficult to distinguish between manuka and kanuka, a close relative that can grow much higher (up to fifty feet), with smaller flowers, and rather more rare as a honey-producing tree. (It does, however, protect the slower-growing canopy species such as totara and rimu.) The bees know the difference, of course, and if we take the trouble to smell the air, so do we, for the kanuka shrub is not aromatic.

I should also say something in this chapter about wildflowers. There are twenty-one hundred native flowering plants and another eighteen hundred or so species naturalized from overseas. Many of the most lovely of these plants can be seen right down in our bay. The kowhai blossoms I see from the back of my house look like gold earrings hanging from the tree. When we first came, we marked off the border between the lawn of our house and the public lawn a few feet from the beach with New Zealand flax (harakeke) because we like the heavy, stout stems, which can burst into bright red flowers with coal-black seeds. They grow at great speed and now, just two years after planting them, act like a semitransparent wall. We like them because the plant has been in New Zealand for millions of years. As soon as they landed, the Maori discovered they could use them to weave baskets and bind their canoes. You can find mountain flax (wharariki) growing when practically nothing else can—in nutrient-starved soils, for example.

Our roof garden bursts into bloom every spring with native ice plants (*Disphyma australe*), which despite the name should not be confused with the Australian ice plant, which has smaller purple flowers, a coastal plant that is endemic to New Zealand, with its beautiful white and deep pink flowers on little fat bubbly green stalks. The many "volunteer" grasses that have made our roof their home do not displease me in the least. I love that you can now see little green gardens growing on three levels of our roofs when you swim out to sea or even just walk by the house on the beach.

I am partial to the naturalized nasturtiums, with their saucer leaves and orange flowers, that grow wild all over our bay, and that I love to add to our salads. I enjoy seeing the kahili ginger plants (*Hedychium gardnerianum*) with their reddish orange, spiderlike flowers.

People here hate the small-flowered nightshade (*Solanum americanum*) because it is toxic. Fair enough, but it is nonetheless lovely to look at, with its delicate white flowers with a tiny yellow stem that resembles a potato (it is a member of the potato family, after all) and the perfect black sphere of the ripe fruit.

As for feral fruit, is it not one of the pleasures of life to make a fruit salad of blackberry, gooseberry, strawberry, and raspberry, all feral, growing wild in the countryside?

Humans are attracted primarily to the color of wildflowers, but it is good for our collective human ego to be reminded that many insects and birds see colors we cannot perceive at all, for they are in the UV range of light wavelengths. Proof, if such were needed, that flowers did not evolve for our eyes, but to attract birds and insects to carry their genes and hereditary information afield, long before any humans were on earth.

*L*iving in New Zealand offers a unique opportunity to reacquaint oneself with trees: There are some fourteen hundred flowering plants here, and two-thirds of these are not seen anywhere else. Richard St. Barbe Baker, the environmentalist who began what may have been the first international conservation movement, the "Men of the Trees," notes that the "primitive New Zealand forest is unlike any other temperate forest, in that it is classed with that tropical type known as 'rain forest.' " The true rain forest in New Zealand (there is one just half an hour from Auckland) has a dense undergrowth of ferns, mosses, and lichens, as well as tangled vines and lianas, and looks impenetrable. But just about any forest on the North Island tends to be lush and abounds in many species of tree ferns and an equal number of soft bright green mosses. Moreover, the number of epiphytes that look like giant grass nests perched on many of the trunks and branches of the tall trees give just about any forest a primeval look. Some of the most immense trees in New Zealand, like the rata, themselves began life as perching epiphytes upon a host tree. Standing below one of these giant trees and looking up to see hundreds of epiphytes is awe inspiring and not a little frightening, since some of them weigh hundreds of pounds; should they pry loose and fall, the result could be deadly.

When I have visited the German countryside, also rich in trees, for some reason I failed to have the nearly numinous experience around trees that I routinely have here. Have I evolved, or is it that New Zealand offers a greater variety, or am I just more susceptible to the kinds of trees that flourish by the ocean? I am not alone. Just about all visitors to New Zealand quickly become enchanted with the most colorful of all seaside plants, the pohutukawa tree (*Metrosideros excelsa*). It is also known as the New Zealand Christmas tree because of its red blossoms that appear in December, a tree related to guavas, feijoas, eucalyptus, and all members of the myrtle family. Possibly the single most sacred tree in New Zealand is found at the tip of the North Island, at Cape Reinga: a small pohutukawa that the

Maori say has been there for eight hundred years. It guards the entrance to a sacred cave through which the disembodied spirits of the dead pass on their way to the next world. To reach our house you have to go through a forest of several dozen large pohutukawa trees, with their silvery gnarled trunks and age-bent branches, and when you finally reach the sea, there is one old fella in particular whose large roots go right out into the ocean. This glorious, wise-looking old tree has been here hundreds of years and may be one of the reasons that the Treaty of Waitangi was signed in our bay, right beneath it. Children climb its giant branches, and our cats spend part of every day racing along the various trunks. Whenever I drive along the coast, I see pohutukawas in the most precarious situations, clinging, it would seem, for dear life, to the very edge of a cliff, half of their root system exposed to the waves of the sea. But then you realize the tree has been there for hundreds of years—that it *wants* to be there (if I can be excused the anthropomorphic term). It seems to *like* being at the edge of the sea. I like to fancy that there is a special relationship between the ocean and this hardy tree. The salt-laden winds that batter its branches seem to give it pleasure, and whether there is rain or not hardly seems to make a difference to this tough old bird. It can be loved too much: The much-hated Australian possum has developed a taste for the nectar and fresh shoots of the pohutukawa, and the trees have begun a steady decline. Humans, too, have a tendency to park their cars right on top of the sensitive root system and even to tear off its branches for firewood. Project Crimson is a wonderful attempt on the part of the DOC to reverse the fortunes of this wondrous tree, and more than seventy thousand have been planted since the early 1990s.

Size matters in trees. So does age. Walking through the redwood forests in Northern California, especially at Muir Woods just north of San Francisco, instills a sense of humility: to think that some of these trees have been there for more than a thousand years. *What must they "know"?* you cannot help but think. The same feeling comes over me whenever I visit kauri groves here, which is often. Kauri trees (*Agathis australis*) are certainly unrivaled in New Zealand for their size and grandeur. They have been here for more than 130 million years, changing hardly at all in that time. Driving up the northern coast, we stopped in the Waipoua Forest to visit Tane Mahuta, Lord of the Forest, the single largest living kauri tree in New Zealand. Large, distinguished trees were often given individual names by Maori. This glorious tree rises to nearly 160 feet, with a girth of almost 40 feet. Though nobody knows how old it is, it was probably a mature tree when Caesar was invading England before the birth of Christ. The oldest kauri, given the name of Kairaru by the Maori, was destroyed by fire in 1886. This Northland kauri was estimated to be at least four thousand years old! Three times the size of Tane Mahuta, Kairaru has been called the single "largest tree in the world," and the claim was made that a full score (twenty) houses could have been built from this one specimen. The average-size single kauri tree contains as much timber as three acres of good spruce forest in middle Europe.

When we stood in front of Tane Mahuta and looked up,

everyone present fell completely silent. For most people, awe is the only possible emotion when faced with this living giant. Not everyone experienced this emotion, however. As has happened with almost every other large tree in the world, people who first saw it had greed in their hearts, not wonder. Its hardwood timber was coveted throughout the world and was extensively logged. Whereas kauri forests once covered at least three million acres, today they have been reduced to a mere two hundred thousand. True, the Maori also felled the trees for use in building their canoes, carving, and building of maraes, but in much smaller numbers. Since the trees held a high rank in Maori thinking, each felling was accompanied by an elaborate community ritual. Cutting down such a tree was a momentous event, not to be undertaken lightly or for purely personal gain. A particularly grand tree would be considered a rakau rangatira, a "chiefly tree" similar in status to a rangatira human. Moreover, if ancestors were buried under a particular tree, it became sacred, even tapu ("taboo"), and could not be cut down. (The Maori preferred to put a dead body in the hollow of a large tree, such as a puriri, but the kauri was so hard it was rarely found hollow and so the bodies were buried underneath the tree rather than inside it.) Nor, of course, did the Maori ever export trees to a foreign market. When the first settlers arrived, though the Maori had cut down trees for hundreds of years for their homes and their canoes, there was no lack of large, majestic kauri. The situation soon changed. No early settler ever had any of the sentimental attachment (in the best sense of both words) with which almost every Maori was blessed.

The resin of this tree is known as kauri gum and was already used by the Maori for starting a fire and as a chewing gum. The soot from the burned gum was used in the tattooing process. It was much sought after in the nineteenth century as a shellac for ships and a slow-drying varnish with a hard finish (and later in the making of linoleum and as a polish). The trouble is that a kauri would produce about three or four pounds of naturally exuded gum a year, but if it was "bled," it could produce up to fifty pounds. It was realized only fairly recently by the Department of Forests that bleeding injured trees. In 1899 an astonishing 11,116 tons of gum were exported from New Zealand, the highest export for any year. A well-known botanist, Leonard Cockayne, writing in 1908 about the Waipoua Forest, says: "[that] this treatment is injurious to the trees goes without saying. Leaving the loss of the sap out of the question, the openings allow the incursion of fungi inimical to the tree, and rotting wood in abundance soon shows the damage that is being done, while dead trees, alive and healthy only a few years before, testify to the rapidity of their action." After all the gum that was lying about the roots of the trees was used up, and after all the large masses formed in the forks of the branches were taken, the only thing left was to dig up the older gum, often clear pieces of fossilized gum. I have seen pale lemon-yellow pieces (or reddish brown ones) with embedded cones or leaves that are as beautiful as any piece of jewelry.

Up to six thousand "diggers" (usually from Yugoslavia) worked on the Northland gum fields. The money was good, since there was no rent to pay—they lived in small huts they built themselves in the forest. One of the men, A. H. Reed, who later became an authority on the kauri, wrote of the independence and romance of the job, how a digger's "days were spent out on the hills, or flats, or swamps, spade and spear in hand, pouch strapped on his side . . . at night he sat by candle-light, jack-knife in hand, scraping the dirt off his gum to make it saleable." Much of the land, however, was left despoiled and useless, where once the mighty forests of kauri had stood for millions of years. On the outskirts of Waipoua even today, writes Richard St. Barbe Baker, "there are many sorry examples of this melancholy desolation of our making where prey at will the sun and wind and rain"—in other words, where the protection of these giants are gone. He reminds us of A. E. Housman's line: "Where trees are fallen, there is grief." A kauri forest, of which, alas, there are few left, was an important habitat for birds and other animals. Rare animals, such as the brown kiwi and the elusive Hochstetter's frog, lived in these forests, as did the kaka parrot.

I find no tree more beautiful here than the puriri (pronounced with a long *u*, and the emphasis on the first syllable), or *Vitex lucens*, a relative of the teak tree. It is a tall tree, growing up to about sixty feet and five feet in diameter. It produces attractive tubular red-pink flowers and bright red fruit all year long, which means that many birds love to sit in its branches, especially the kereru, the native wood pigeon, but also nectar eaters such as the tui and bellbirds. The tree is much prized by the Maori for medicinal purposes: Water from the boiled leaves is traditionally used for backache, and the infusion for ulcers and sore throats. What I find especially appealing is to see one of these huge trees in the forest with every large branch densely loaded with nest epiphytes, which look like the large nests made by storks in Europe. These lily-related, dark green nest epiphytes have long narrow leaves tufted in large clumps, with funnel-like spaces between the leaf bases that are able to store large amounts of rainwater. They look like hanging gardens, and indeed, they sustain hosts of insects and birds, and can sometimes be of enormous size and weight. They appear to me to be sustainers of life, and are a symbol of the richness of forest life. When Ilan was just four, he learned the word *epiphyte* and he loved to instruct fellow hikers. It has a nice feel to it in the mouth and feels somehow commensurate with the lovely object of which it acts as the symbol.

Karaka Bay derives its name from the trees so common here, the karaka (*Corynocarpus laevigatus*), perhaps the most important tree to the Maori of all native trees—so important that it's claimed this tree was introduced with the first canoe to arrive in New Zealand from the Pacific (I saw them in New Caledonia). It is, in fact, one of the few trees that the Maori actually cultivated, for the kernel was one of the staple articles of the Maori diet. They loved the orange berries, poisonous if eaten raw. They would place them in water, and to remove the outer pulp would pound them with their feet; the kernels were cooked in an earth oven for twenty-four hours, and then placed in water until eaten. This removed the toxic glycoside, which when consumed can even lead to death. They were not always successful in their treatment of the berries, however, since karaka poisoning was a common form of death for the Maori. The Maori also wore the leaves on their head when they visited the graves of their ancestors, often taken from (tapu) karaka groves they planted. We have a beautiful, large karaka tree just outside our bedroom window, and I am waiting for it to attract the iridescent giant native pigeon, the kereru, which likes to feed on the berries and is evidently immune to their toxic effect. Strange, isn't it, how native peoples find poisonous species attractive, and learn to avoid the poison? Perhaps the principle is that something so powerful must have beneficial effects as well, if only we can find them. The Maori did this with the toxic tutu plant (actually a tree, the *Coriaria arborea*), whose berries contain tutin, a highly toxic poison. (A close relative is used in witchcraft rituals in Chile.) Horses and cattle, left to graze in a paddock that contains spreading tutu, can die from it (so-called toot poisoning). The trick is to avoid the poisonous seeds, squeezing the berries and filtering the juice. The leaves were used by the Maori for healing cuts and bruises, and the root in various medicinal ways—as a cure for neuralgia, rheumatism, and more.

The mighty totara (*Podocarpus totara*), unique to New Zealand, which looks something like the American redwood, is another tree highly esteemed by the Maori. Its bark is used for medicinal purposes, including fever and skin complaints, and the wood of the trunk itself is often used for the great war canoes. (It is apparently the only timber capable of resisting attacks of shipworm, a marine boring mollusk.) Canoes capable of holding a hundred warriors were made from a single totara trunk. It also produces a huge amount of fruit, a nutlike berry that changes from green through yellow to red (when mature, the seeds are black), which was eaten by the Maori. So important was the tree that fine healthy trees were considered heirlooms owned by individual families. Dispute about the possession of such trees actually led to wars. The reddish hue of the wood was considered the color most appropriate to royalty, which only added to its luster as a sacred tree. The tree is large, averaging ninety feet when full grown. The wood is so durable that tree trunks that have lain in the earth for hundreds of years can still be used for building and fencing. Alas, most of the great totara have already been felled and only a few giant specimens remain, such as the 120-foot-tall tree near Pureora Forest in the central North Island, near Lake Taupo.

The kahikatea (*Dacrycarpus dacrydioides*), also called white pine, is the tallest of New Zealand's native trees; it can reach heights of more than two hundred feet and live for five or more centuries! People here refer to kahikatea forests as dinosaur forests, because they existed at the same time as the dinosaurs. That is a humbling thought: They were here long before any humans roamed the earth. The tree also produces a prodigious amount of fruit; sometimes a single individual can bear almost two thousand pounds of fruit, which attract the kereru, bell-bird, and tui, who flock to its richly laden branches. Maori eat the red berries upon which the fruit sits. (The berry is formed from the scales that bear the fruit.) Something about this bounty makes it feel to me like a kind of generosity of spirit, as if this tree is offering something valuable to the world. How can one talk about the "wisdom" of a tree, or apply human terms like *generosity?*—and yet somehow it feels right. Just as it feels wrong—very wrong, to me—that these great sentient beings (there is, after all, no dispute that they are alive) should be cut down, a kind of murder almost, for products that are not essential to our existence, such as disposable chopsticks. Once a particular tree, one that has lived for hundreds of years in the same spot, is gone, that tree is gone forever. How can we be comfortable with that?

Is it any better if the trees are cultivated specifically to be cut down? Sustainable cultivation, it is called, and I can see the argument in its favor. In California I was fond of a tree called the Monterey pine. More than 3.5 million acres of New Zealand are planted in what is called "exotic forest," though there is nothing exotic about it to me, since of that, 90 percent is radiata pine (*Pinus radiata*), otherwise known as Monterey pine. (Its total habitat in California is only 17,500 acres.) When I saw these trees growing here in enormous profusion, I felt rather sad. They looked out of place. I know that the impulse behind the plantings, which are now the mainstay of the New Zealand timber industry, was a good one—to preserve native forests from being logged out. I saw them growing near Rotorua, where conditions are somewhat similar to their natural habitat in California (more or less the same latitude, too), and they grow twice as large there as they do in California (more than 120 feet). Still, something did not feel right, almost as if these trees had been captured, taken from their native country, and transplanted (literally) in a foreign land not for their own benefit, but to satisfy greed. Somehow I could not get the idea of slavery out of my mind (even though I know it sounds absurd to make such a comparison). Walking through such forests, I missed native birds and signs of life on the forest floor. Everything felt slightly empty, almost artificial. The awful sight of denuded hills left me feeling equally desolate. I hope I am not being oversentimental. Actually, I know I am not: A wound is a wound; why should not a mountain be wounded?

*R*imu (*Dacrydium cupressinum*) is another native podocarp—evergreen, important timber trees belonging to the yew family, with sixty species. Resembling totara, kahikatea, and various pine trees, the rimu is a particularly graceful tree and can reach immense heights (up to 150 feet), though it does not seem as majestic to me as its close cousin, the kahikatea. When young, its leaves are pendulous, almost like weeping willows, but they are much longer-lived, resembling, rather, the great redwoods of North America. Its heart is so filled with resin that Maori use the wood for torches. These trees are now the mainstay of the native timber market and are being felled at a terrible rate. It is estimated that by 2006, when clear-felling (which simply means cutting down all the trees from a specific area in a single operation) is to stop, perhaps a hundred thousand rimu trees will have been cut down. When you see the bald spot on the mountain from where they are gone, it resembles a giant abcess. It is not a pretty sight.

When we first arrived in New Zealand, I was sure we were on a tropical island, because wherever I looked, I saw palm trees. What I was seeing was the nikau (*Rhopalostylis sapida*), the southernmost palm tree in the Southern Hemisphere. It is the only native palm tree in New Zealand. Never more than about thirty feet tall, it is a slow-growing tree, taking thirty years to burst into an inflorescence of small pink flowers (with ripe red berries from the previous season equally visible; these take a year to ripen and are loved by the native pigeon and other birds, who feast on them in the summer). You can actually count the years of any given tree by adding up the very visible ringed horizontal leaf scars on its trunk and adding twenty-five years, which is how long it takes before the first such ring appears. I never realized, when I was visiting Brazil, that the hearts of (coconut) palm salad I was so fond of involved killing the entire tree—cutting out its heart, not surprisingly, causes the tree to die. Something similar happens to the nikau when its "heart" of undeveloped leaves is harvested. (The Maori eat the green berries, which does not appear to harm the tree.) The shoots of the tree taste a bit like artichokes, and are much prized by the Maori. Strands of nikau on a beach are a potent reminder for me of Hawaii, especially when the sun is setting and you see the silhouette of the palms against the evening sky.

Another tree that gives Auckland a tropical look and feel is the cabbage tree (*Cordyline australis*), related to the magnificent

Joshua trees in the Southern California desert, and part of the lily family group. It is called ti kouka by the Maori and is much loved: The Maori eat and make drinks from its roots, stems, and leaf buds; they make kete (baskets) and thatch their houses from the leaves (at least in the past, when they lived in small villages); they use it for medicinal purposes against colic, dysentery, and diarrhea; and, after a baby is born, the placenta is buried under special cabbage trees. The five species of this tree are unique to New Zealand, though it probably arrived from Asia some fifteen million years ago. The tree fascinates people because it has the fabled property of indestructibility. There is some truth to this: Years ago a Northland gum digger used the hollow tree trunks of the cabbage tree to make a chimney in his hut. There was a constant fire for several months, but after the man left, neighbors noticed green shoots growing out of the cambium. This is not a unique occurrence. Even if the trees are found uprooted on a beach and soaked through for a year with salt water, they can be planted and will come back to life. This is because on its rhizome (the underground stem also known as a rootstalk), there are thousands of buds that can sprout into a whole tree. It is not, however, invasive, and nobody would ever object to the sudden appearance of this beautiful tree. The cover of this book shows a stand of cabbage trees in the Milford Sound. Any New Zealander seeing such a stand when out of the country is instantly homesick.

Continuing the theme of my mistaking Auckland for Hawaii, there are no fewer than forty-four species of ferns found only in New Zealand (of more than two hundred species altogether, out of ten thousand species worldwide). Some are so tall they look like trees, giving the city and its surroundings a decidedly island flavor. The two most common and most beautiful are the silver tree fern or ponga (*Cyathea dealbata*), and the mamaku (*C. medullaris*). The first is the national symbol of New Zealand. It derives its name from the fact that the underside of the fronds is a light silver color. Often somebody blazing a trail will lay down ponga, silver-side up, a highly visible indication of the correct path. The second, the Mamaku, is my personal favorite. It is New Zealand's tallest tree fern, growing to a height of forty-five feet, with a dark black trunk. Its uncurled new shoots (the koru shape of the fern is a central motif for many New Zealand logo designs) look like small babies asleep. (Maori eat the new shoots as a delicacy.) When we placed "dead" logs around our vegetable garden, we were surprised a few weeks later to see miniature fern trees sprouting up all along the logs. Several dozen came to life within a matter of weeks and surrounded our vegetables, something that seems to gladden everyone's heart.

It is also a delight for me to walk along the main street above our house and see lichens growing on the pavement and sometimes right on the street itself. The bright colors (some a vivid orange) are like a visible sign of the health they advertise for the entire environment. Lichens are like the proverbial miner's canary: They grow only where there is no pollution. Seeing them in such myriad forms and so profuse makes me feel good about living where I do. Actually, New Zealand has one of the richest collections of lichens in the world, with almost a thousand species already described. Some of the lichen growing on rocks can be as old as forty-five hundred years!

I have spoken here only of native trees, but I must confess that I have become infatuated with a foreigner. I have fallen in love with the Australian Morton Bay fig tree. Perhaps this comes from my days in Adyar, near Madras in the south of India, when I was a boy of fifteen. I saw what is arguably the world's largest tree, a banyan tree (*Ficus religiosus*) under which an entire village can gather. While the Morton Bay fig trees here are not quite that large, they are still enormous, at least fifty feet tall, with root systems that resemble the thighs of elephants, large, powerful, and with an ivory-white sheen. The wild figs are not edible, but these giant trees exude a kind of majesty that is irresistible to me.

Another confession: I love banana stands; on our beach there are several, and banana trees seem to grow easily here, right next to the ocean, although they, too, are an introduced species. They also produce delicious, tiny yellow bananas that Manu, our son, loves to eat. Papaya trees, too, proliferate on the beach, and they have the most beautiful of all trunks, a bit like the trunk of an elephant, with a wonderful feel to them, solid yet delicate, powerful yet graceful. I never tire of looking at them. I also enjoy the many citrus trees on our beach, and the large magnolia trees up the hill that bloom even before spring. I have a soft spot for the avocado orchards, which harks back to when I first saw them growing in Ojai, California. It is not only that I am addicted to the fruit; I also love the tree itself, so dense, giving such perfect shade, a bit like the magnificent mango tree (which, alas, does not grow here).

New Zealand has been isolated from the rest of the land-masses of the world for millions of years now. Jared Diamond, a University of California—Los Angeles biologist, has said, "New Zealand is as close as we will get to the opportunity to study life on another planet." The fact that New Zealand was isolated for so long means that any animals that were here al-ready were often to be found in their most primitive form, speaking from a purely chronological point of view. They have not evolved in millions of years. The most famous of these is the tuatara (Maori for "spiny back")—a reptile so old that it was here when dinosaurs were also evolving, making the tu-atara the oldest representative of its kind still alive. It looks much like a lizard, but isn't one. A slow-moving, unexcitable animal, it can live up to a hundred years. Juveniles are not ma-ture until they are thirteen years old, and do not reach their full size until they are nearly thirty-five. Even the eggs (all nineteen of them) are slow to hatch: It takes them almost as long as an elephant, up to sixteen months! There are perhaps a hundred thousand tuatara in the whole of New Zealand, but none at all on the mainland. They are all found on offshore islands (twenty-five of them, off Whangarei in the Hauraki Gulf, and off Coromandel), and I have yet to meet anybody who has seen one in nature. One of the great mysteries of biology, which makes the tuatara fascinating to scientists, is the third eye growing on the top of its head. It is connected to the pineal gland and seems to act as a biological clock, but nobody is certain of its exact function.

When I was young, frogs fascinated me. I enjoyed visiting Fern Dell, not far from our house in the Hollywood Hills, where thousands of frogs lived in small ponds that lined a gently sloping hill for several acres. I loved to see the tadpoles slowly transform into little green frogs, and could not resist taking them home to live in a pond I constructed on the hill in our backyard. I had hundreds of them there. Walking to school, I would often see dozens of tiny frogs in the ditches that lined the street, and it gave me a curious kind of comfort to know these minuscule creatures were there, living their lives so close to mine, yet so distinct from mine. I look for frogs wherever I go, and found that when I was living in France I could be flung into a state of despair by learning that local frogs wound up on the menu. I never ate a frog and could not imagine ever doing so.

When I came to New Zealand, I was sure I would see (or at least hear) thousands of frogs. I did not. In fact, in the three years I have been here, I have never seen a single native frog. That upsets me. People tell me that they see frogs all the time, though what they see are introduced tree frogs from Australia—the whistling frog and the golden bell frog (so called because it can produce a tinkling sound), green with golden yellowish bands along the back and down each side of the body. The native frogs here are the same frogs, unchanged, who were here more than 135 million years ago. In this, they resemble the tuatara. There are only three species of native frogs, and all three are endangered. No wonder I have never seen one. In the Coromandel Peninsula is Archey's frog (*Leiopelma archeyi*); in the areas near Auckland is Hochstetter's frog (*L. hochstetteri*), which may number just a few thousand in all; and finally there are just two hundred Hamilton's frogs, on a single island (Stephens Island in the Cook Strait). None of these frogs has ears, none of them croaks, and none of them goes through a tadpole stage. They are born as tiny froglets, first inhabiting a miniature pond of their own (the egg sac, filled with water); when they hatch they climb onto their father's (!) back and spend their final week of development with him. They can then live for almost a quarter century!

In November 1852 an army surgeon, Arthur Saunders Thomson, was nearby when gold diggers were washing rocks in a stream in the mountains of the Coromandel. Under one of the boulders, they found a frog. "When they saw me they gave me the animal. I took it to the place where Lieutenant-Governor Wynard was holding a conference with the tribes for the purpose of making a treaty to enable the Europeans to dig gold. The frog was shown to many of the natives and was carefully examined by several intelligent old men. None of these individuals had ever seen the animal before, nor could they give any name to it. All the New Zealanders [Maori] present were much struck by its appearance, and they said it be the *atua*, the spirit of god of the gold, which had appeared on the earth; many of them shrunk back from it in horror, and some of them were inclined to draw unfavorable omens from its discovery at such a particular time." So it would appear the Maori did not know of the existence of frogs, and as far as I know there is no word for "frog" in Maori. People in the Coromandel call these frogs "the Little Red Men" because they have green flecks mingled with light reddish brown ones. I'm convinced the Maori's instinctive revulsion had little to do with the frog and everything to do with the way their land and its inhabitants were being treated by the settlers.

Many scientists have debunked the idea that the vanishing frog population—or frogs born with mysterious limb abnormalities—portends some kind of serious problem with the quality of the environment. Still, I find the thesis entirely plausible. After all, frogs have extremely sensitive skin, and it is not surprising that an ozone hole four times as large as Australia would affect them just as it affects us. My direct experience has been that anywhere I used to see many frogs when I was younger, in that same place I now see many fewer. Whatever the cause, it makes me sad, for something lovely is less common in our world. I do not like to think that I shall have to one day explain to a little boy or girl what a frog looks like.

I cannot close this chapter without discussing what is perhaps my favorite New Zealand animal: the eel, *Anguilla dieffenbachia.* The marine biologist Tony Ayling of the University of Auckland has been studying the long-finned New Zealand eel for years and feels we have barely begun to understand their mysteries. They can be very large: A female can weigh over a hundred pounds and be six feet long. They can be very old as well: Don Jellyman of the National Institute of Water and Atmospheric Research has found eels in Lake Rotoiti, just east of Rotorua on the North Island, with an estimated age of more than a hundred years. In fact, the average age of the eels from this lake was ninety-four. They normally live in an inland river or lake for as long as thirty-five years before they begin, between March and May, what will turn into a three-thousand-mile journey. During this time they cease to eat, and even their physical shape undergoes a sea change: Their eyes grow large in order to see in the dim light of the ocean depths, which is where they travel and which is also their goal. They swim to tropical seas near Samoa and Tonga where they spawn, males and females mating, at depths of twelve thousand feet! Then both adults die. The thousands of leaflike larvae swim for more than a year before beginning their yearlong return journey to New Zealand. Just as a duck imprints on a mother duck, these tiny eelets have genetically imprinted on fresh water, and are able to "smell" when they have reached a freshwater river. There they undergo a further transformation: into transparent "glass" eels, climbing waterfalls and dams, up to the same river where their mother lived. This can take as long as seven years. During this time the glass eel undergoes its final metamorphosis, losing its transparency, becoming dark, developing a stomach and intestines, and is now officially known as an "elver." Thirty to a hundred years later, the grown eels begin the whole sequence again. With such a life cycle, no wonder the Maori consider them to be the progeny of supernatural beings. (They also take them to be a taonga, "traditional treasure.")

When I was visiting the Coromandel, some young friends of our family, the delightful Georgia and Martin Carr, knew of my interest in animals and took me on a hike up Driving Creek Stream (where gold was discovered in 1840) to a certain spot in the river where there was a small pond and a tiny cave under a rock. They called out "Ellie! Ellie!" and, after a while, a large female long-finned eel emerged from the cave and took some luncheon meat from the hand of one of the kids. Eventually she brought her whole large body out on the rocks and allowed us to touch her amazing skin; I was even able to lift her up. Clearly, this eel actually trusted us. How odd: A completely wild animal makes the distinction, one we think is beyond the capacity of a beast, between humans she can trust and others she cannot. The children who took me there warned me: If a hunter finds her, he will take a shovel and slice her in two. You must never tell! The eel trusts the children because she knows they have an innocence that most adults have lost. She would not come out for a long time while I was there. She is blind, and took her time testing the air with her powerful sense of smell. I passed the test, and how proud I felt.

*I*t is strange, at sixty-three, to be discovering that I have a passion for flora and fauna! Is it because New Zealand is such an extraordinary place, or is it just that I am now mature enough, and perhaps have slowed down enough, to pause and take a long look around? I suddenly realize that I am not alone, that I live surrounded by other living beings, most of whom are not human. I heard birds all my life, but I am just beginning to see them; I saw trees all my life, but I think I am just beginning to hear them. I owe a debt of gratitude to this strange and ancient land I now call home.

For Further Reading
Much of the information for this chapter was taken from an outstanding book, *The Natural World of New Zealand* by Gerard Hutching. Auckland: Penguin, 1998.

Another excellent book is by Tim Flannery, the director of the South Australian Museum in Sydney, *The Future Eaters: An Ecological History of the Australasian Lands and People.* New York: Grove Press, 1994.

Also useful was Richard St. Barbe Baker's *Famous Trees of New Zealand.* Wellington: A. H. Reed, 1965. Baker founded the "Men of the Trees" movement, was active in the reforestation of the Sahara, and was requested by Presidents Roosevelt and Kennedy to take a lead in the preservation of the giant redwoods of coastal California.

Finally, I got useful tips about wildflowers from an excellent book by Peter Johnson, *Pick of the Bunch: New Zealand Wildflowers.* Dunedin: Longacre Press, 1997.

chapter 6

The Trouble with Paradise

*T*he photograph on the cover of this book depicts a paradise. I have chosen to use this word in the title of this book. Of course there is always trouble in paradise, and New Zealand is no exception. But many of the problems I have encountered here can be turned on their head to be seen as virtues. Such, for example, are the stroppy poppy choppers. There is something nice in the fact that New Zealanders resent somebody who thinks he is better or smarter than somebody else. I find this refreshing. America, and Europe too, yield far too quickly to the expert, to authority. I have written an entire book (*Against Therapy*) trying to show that the idea of expertise when it comes to the human emotions—for example, love, disappointment, sadness, joy—is absurd. None of us knows more about these matters than anyone else. I think most Kiwis are inclined to agree. In fact, they are inclined to take it even farther: I have no problem reaching out for an expert plumber or electrician, whereas most Kiwis feel they can do this themselves. When we first moved into our house I asked our neighbors for the number of a good handyman. Raised eyebrows all around. *You* are your own handyperson here, mate!

When I used the word *paradise* to describe New Zealand, I was thinking of the original Persian use of the term, where paradise was an enclosed and protected orchard, a park, and a garden. This suits New Zealand fine. The Bible uses the word to refer to the Garden of Eden. But there is no such idyllic place on earth now. So New Zealand is not a paradise of that sort.

I have not failed to notice problems here, as there are problems everywhere. If I draw attention to some of the ways in which New Zealand fails to be a paradise, it is not to carp or complain, but in the hope of finding clarification, explanation, and encouraging change.

*T*he rates of depression and of suicide are as high here as just about anyplace on earth. Of course sadness knows no passport restrictions, no nationality, and, worst of all, it does not respond to the most natural form of all therapies, being exposed to natural beauty. All the beauty of the New Zealand landscape becomes irrelevant when you are confined, whether physically or in your own mind. Consider the beautiful passage by Janet Frame, New Zealand's best-known writer, from *To the Is-Land* (describing her feelings when she was just three): "I remember a grey day when I stood by the gate and listened to the wind in the telegraph wires. I had my first conscious feeling of an outside sadness, or it seemed to come from outside, from the sound of the wind moaning in the wires. I looked up and down the white dusty road and saw no one. The wind was blowing from place to place past us, and I was there, in between, listening. I felt a burden of sadness and loneliness as if something had happened or begun and I knew about it."

Physical beauty does not seem to make any difference in depression, perhaps because the landscape appears indifferent to you, which in some sense it is. The landscape does not change when you commit suicide. New Zealand has one of the highest suicide rates in the world, especially for young people between the ages of fifteen and twenty-four. In 1999 there were 119 suicides, that is, 30 per 100,000. We always think we know the causes of suicide, but we rarely do. In the United States a man in his thirties who jumped off the Golden Gate Bridge in San Francisco left behind a note that read: "I'm going to walk to the bridge. If one person smiles at me on the way I will not jump." He jumped. If you smile and say hello to people in New Zealand, it is highly unlikely that even a single one will not respond in kind, and yet the suicide rate is still high. One wonders, though, if a youth who commits suicide does so on a momentary impulse that would cease the next moment, if only he or she had waited. One severely depressed man who survived after jumping from the Golden Gate Bridge in 1985 said that as he fell he "instantly realized that everything in my life that I'd thought was unfixable was totally fixable except for having just jumped."

In Finland, I thought I understood suicide. There was no light. There was, I thought, such a simple solution: light therapy. I was wrong. New Zealand has natural light therapy and yet a high suicide rate. In fact, Pacific Island societies have as much suicide as the cold, bleak northern countries, and in certain places, at certain times, such as Samoa in the 1990s, there can be suicidal peaks despite the great natural beauty. As one Maori woman said to me recently when I told her the title of this book: "Well, it may be a paradise to you and other white people like you, but to the tangata whenua, 'original inhabitants,' it is something less. Much less. You have stolen our land." I was embarrassed, instantly realizing her words were true. I was wrong to think that the weather explained the sadness that I saw so often in Finland. True, there were literally hundreds of Finnish words for variations on sadness and depression. Positive words, words of comfort, of joy and love, were much less commonly used. A woman told me it was not unusual for a married couple to live their entire marriage without ever once saying, "I love you." But I am afraid that this interesting observation (not original with me) could not all be laid at the feet of the cold dark winters of Northern Europe, much as it would satisfy me were this true. In fact, nobody in New Zealand understands the high rates of suicide, and the puzzle remains for the moment unsolved. Comparative suicidology (I know, it is an awful word) is attempting to understand high suicide rates around the world in a comparative light, and I think this is an important undertaking. There may not be any easy or simple answers, however. Neither sociology nor psychology seems able to understand this puzzling phenomenon.

*T*here are serious health problems here. New Zealand once ranked third best for child health in the world. Now it is twenty-sixth. The rates of TB, rheumatic fever, meningitis, and more, are high—so high they can be compared to the rates of third-world countries, a humiliating fact to many New Zealanders. Ian Hassall, a pediatrician and New Zealand's first commissioner for children, has said: "We are out of sorts with our children. They are abused and neglected and kill themselves in numbers that compare unfavorably with other countries. We fail to provide effective services for them and their families. Our society is unbalanced. We are sowing the seeds of discord, dysfunction, and national decline."

Why are children suffering in this way? The explanation is not far to seek: All these diseases are related to crowded housing and so, ultimately, to poverty. New migrants, especially from the Pacific Islands, are forced by poverty to live in very crowded conditions—conditions ideal for an outbreak of TB, or the current meningitis epidemic in New Zealand. There are many people in Auckland who do not have enough money to feed their children. From 1997 to 2001 the Auckland City Mission food bank has seen a 140 percent increase in the number of food parcels it issues. Children are the first to suffer the effects of poverty. There is no official poverty line here, unlike in the United States and Britain, but we do know that poverty has been increasing in New Zealand, especially since 1991, when benefits were, for political reasons, substantially cut. When a person is earning sixteen thousand New Zealand dollars a year (about ten thousand U.S.), and when 50 percent of that is spent on housing (even state housing has been deregulated in the 1990s to conform to market pressures), how can anyone expect the children in these families to live a healthy life? They cannot even eat fruits and vegetables because their families cannot afford them.

More than half of all children born in the mid- to late 1990s have been exposed to the benefit system—that is, their parents, or even more likely, a single parent, is forced to rely on benefits (called here DPB, domestic purpose benefits, which by definition means a parent caring for a child without a partner). Maori are two and a half times more likely to live in poverty, and Pacific Islanders three and a half times more so than Pakeha, or New Zealanders of European descent. It seems that at least 20 percent of all people in New Zealand could be defined as poor. And when they say *poor* here, they really mean it: sixteen New Zealand dollars a day (about ten dollars U.S.) to feed a family of five! Thirty-three percent of all New Zealand children live in poor households, and 72 percent of single-parent families exist below the estimated poverty line. If somebody is living on domestic purpose benefits, about $225 New Zealand a week, they will almost certainly have problems paying for food (77 percent of them, a recent survey showed), they will have to go without meals, and they often will not be able to pay their electricity bill at the end of the year, even if they allow it to accumulate. In fact, only about 66 percent of the lowest-income households have a phone, a car, or a washing machine.

This kind of poverty is the direct result of political policy, as the New Zealand political scientist Brian Easton so convincingly showed in his 1986 book, *Wages and the Poor* (see also his 1989 book, *The Making of Rogernomics*). Many intellectuals here agree, and have done important work to show how the misguided economic policies of the National party, when it was in power from 1990 until 1997 under Prime Minister Jim Bolger, created this situation, which really only changed, if it has, under Prime Minister Helen Clark's Labour government from 1999 to the present. (Actually, the problem began much earlier, under the Labour government of former Auckland barrister David Lange, in 1984.)

Can anything be done about this? Of course it can. In 1996 England made a historic commitment to eliminate child poverty within twenty years, and they are making progress. New Zealand can do it, too. In fact, New Zealand has a history of doing unprecedented things: like being the first country in the world to give women the vote and virtually eliminating homelessness.

*H*ow can New Zealand rank near the top in the Western world for child abuse? There were fifty-five deaths of children under the age of fifteen, and nineteen under the age of one year, due to deliberate abuse in the last year for which statistics were available, 2001. The New Zealand rate of 1.3 child deaths per 100,000 was thirteen times greater than the best rate—that of Spain—said the report. A report by UNICEF released in September 2003—the first-ever attempt to draw a comparative picture of the physical abuse of children in the twenty-seven richest nations of the world (known as the Innocenti Report)—showed that Belgium, the Czech Republic, New Zealand, Hungary, and France have levels four to six times higher than the small group of countries—Spain, Greece, Italy, Ireland, and Norway—that have the lowest incidence of child maltreatment deaths. What is surprising to me is that the perpetrators are first and foremost the biological father (about 41 percent) and the biological mother (about 39 percent); the next highest category is the stepfather (about 11 percent). And the sources of all this violence? First comes poverty. A recent government report in Sweden states: "A weak family economy stands out as the background factor most closely associated with childhood abuse, sexual abuse, and bullying. The worse the family economy, the greater the risk of abuse." Alcohol and drug abuse are obvious sources as well. But perhaps the most important factor of all is whether the culture sanctions physical abuse within the home. In October 2003 the Geneva-based United Nations Committee on the Rights of the Child expressed deep concern that New Zealand has not changed a law allowing parents to use "reasonable" force against their children. The report from the United Nations reminded New Zealand that the Convention on the Rights of the Child requires the protection of children from all forms of violence, which includes corporal punishment in the family. In New Zealand, Section 59 of the 1961 Crimes Act says using reasonable force against a child is permissible. The act reads: "Every parent of a child and every person in the place of a parent of a child is justified in using force by way of correction towards the child, if the force used is reasonable in the circumstances." New Zealand appears to be the only country in the world where the law actually *permits* physical punishment. Anyone can claim, of course, that the force they used was "reasonable," or at least so they thought. Who can say they didn't?

New Zealand needs to rescind the law that allows parents to hit their children. Spanking children is banned by statute in eleven countries, including Israel, Sweden, Finland, Denmark, Norway, Austria, Germany, and, by high court ruling, Italy and Switzerland. Spanking was first banned in Sweden in 1979. (Sweden had already banned physical punishment in schools as early as 1958.) People often say that banning something does nothing to remove it from society. This is simply untrue. If it were not, why would we ban smoking, or have laws that compel us to wear seat belts, or make drunk driving punishable by law? Why have sexual harassment laws? Obviously once something is the law of the land, people think about it in a different way. It does not entirely disappear, but attitudes change, and consequently behavior begins to change as well. In Sweden, when the law was passed, 60 percent were opposed to it. Now, many years later, after seeing how good the law has been (there have been no misuses of it at all), only 6 percent of parents under thirty-five support any kind of physical punishment of children. The same thing has happened in Germany over the last several years. In Italy, Judge Francesco Ippolito of the Italian Supreme Court issued a decision that is now basically the law of the land, outlawing the physical punishment of children for any reason. He noted that just as Italy itself had moved away from fascism, so it must also move away from the concept of the authoritarian father who can physically punish his child at will.

*I*f you are coming to New Zealand to find good opera, ballet, the latest in movies, or wonderful concerts, you are in the wrong country. You are better off staying in Berlin or New York or London. You will not find them here. Now, that does not matter so much to me—not nearly as much as being able to walk in bright sunshine along the ocean shore. So I am very happy. But I know people who yearn for the culture they have left behind. New Zealand is remote; there is no use pretending it isn't. (Among other benefits, the country successfully resists Disneyfication for precisely that reason!) There is much to love about the remoteness. Because New Zealand was the last place in the world to be discovered and settled by humans (unless you include the two poles), it is more like what the world was before humans came into it than any other place that exists. Why that should give me a special frisson of pleasure I do not know, but it undeniably does.

Still, it also means that there is a degree of isolation. Could I live here without the Internet? I doubt it. I get *The New York Times* every morning on my computer, as well as the BBC, French and German newspapers, and numerous magazines and journals. I use Amazon on an almost daily basis to keep up to date, and www.addall.com to build up my library. Our goal is to spend three months each year abroad: one month in the United States, one month in Europe, and one month traveling through Asia. I realize that while this is ideal for me, for a younger family, or for someone who had a more traditional job, it would be difficult.

In the twenty-first century physical isolation can easily be alleviated if you have the time and money. After all, in a mere thirteen hours you can be in Los Angeles, and in Sydney in a matter of three hours. We are isolated, but only relatively speaking. Still, it would be nice if my friends and family could get on a plane from the United States and be here in just a few hours. They would come more often, I know. A whole night aboard a plane still has a forbidding sound to it.

Yet geographic isolation becomes less important every year. Perhaps fifty years ago, everything here had a stale, musty odor, metaphorically speaking, like something left behind. There was a sense that New Zealand was not keeping up with the rest of the world. And so the oldest of English jokes (attributed to Clement Freud) is: "I went to New Zealand, but it was closed." I remember meeting the great Russian linguist Roman Jakobsen at Harvard with a friend, a brilliant musicologist by the name of Allan Keiler, who had just accepted a university position in Washington State. Keiler complained to Jakobsen that he felt he was going somewhere that was "out of it." Jakobsen responded memorably: "Ja, vat I vant to know is vhere is the 'it' of vich it is out?" The same idea is expressed in one of the deepest German Jewish jokes about the Holocaust: Two Jews meet in Berlin right after Hitler is made chancellor. The first says: "I am emigrating." "Where to?" asks the second. "Shanghai," is the answer. "What! So far away?" says the first. The deep and unforgettable answer is: *"Weit von wo?"* ("Far from where?") In other words, why would one want to be in the heart of Europe when the heart of Europe is where they are killing Jews?

So about New Zealand, what, exactly, is closed that is open in the England of Clement Freud? (He was best known to the public, by the way, for his appearance on a TV dog food commercial alongside a bloodhound.) "It" is only a state of mind, and that mind can be just as much at home, and just as profound, in New Zealand as anywhere else on our increasingly tiny globe. That said, there are still many reasons for living in the middle of Europe. Well, perhaps not so much living there as having immediate access to it.

At the beginning of this book I mentioned that when I first arrived, in my eagerness to meet people I went in search of the major public intellectuals. It turned out that nobody I have met here would ever describe him- or herself as an intellectual. It would be like saying "I am brainy." Bad form. I see the point, but the downside of this is that people are reluctant to take up a public stance on a matter of vital interest when the issues are purely ones of ideas. Ronald Chapman, a professor of political science and a mentor of the present prime minister, Helen Clark, put it best when we talked about the difficulty of being an intellectual in New Zealand. "Unacceptable," he said. "Why, people think that bastard uses his brain to think! He's a bloody intellectual.' "

*T*here is, here, a certain indifference to the talents, the new ideas, and the cutting-edge kind of thinking that is going on in other parts of the world. Many friends have told me that they have been away from New Zealand for a year, or even much longer, and returned with brand-new ideas they were eager to communicate to their colleagues, whether in the arts, medicine, or some other branch of science, only to be met with what struck them as deep, almost hostile, indifference. It feels like a morbid and injurious lack of curiosity. It has psychological roots, no doubt, but the important thing is to quickly get rid of it.

New Zealand has just been named by the British-based Transparency International the third least corrupt nation in the world. Number one was Finland, number two Iceland, and tied for third were Denmark and New Zealand (followed by Sweden, Singapore, the Netherlands, and Australia). That is a high achievement. I sometimes wonder, though, if there is an inverse correlation between the willingness to bend rules (as in Italy) and dullness. There is, here, an English legacy of a kind of bleak ordinariness. I am always reminded of it when I read the vapid phrase *good enough mothering,* a popular term first used by the English psychoanalyst Donald Winnicott in an attempt to make parents feel okay about themselves, and relieve them of any guilt that they were not being good parents. It has always bothered me, conjuring up pictures of bleak English small towns with bad weather, bad food, unhappy children, and narrow-minded parents.

The English influence is felt in many ways here, even as it is diminishing day by day (just as it has nearly disappeared in England itself). There is a certain standoffishness, a certain lack of enthusiasm here. Calls are often not returned, something that many Americans complain of. It is, by and large, a very white country. Other ethnicities of course exist here, but they do not really make themselves felt in the culture of everyday life, at least to the degree that they do elsewhere. There are no street markets, no sections of town where all the restaurants and all the shops are from someplace else. The small towns here have a feeling of being much of a muchness, very little variety.

A certain dreariness comes from places that have not yet achieved the sophistication that comes from rich diversity. Even in Auckland (never mind a rural setting), you drive along a beautiful winding road in a friendly suburb that takes you past rain forest. You come to an elevated spot where there is a cluster of shops. The sun is shining hard in the middle of winter. You park, and when you get out you can see the ocean from where you are standing. But the shops are not what you want them to be. You have created a scene in your imagination: There is a little café, with tables right on the edge of the small cliff, looking over the sea. The food is ethnic—Mexican, Thai, Vietnamese, Middle Eastern, Turkish—and it is delicious. The people who made it have just arrived from their own country, and know exactly how to prepare food the old-fashioned way. Alas, alas, that is not what you get here. (Pasifika or Maori cultures don't seem to be in the picture at all, at least in the choice spots where tourists tend to go.)

One of New Zealand's finest writers, John Mulgan, died in 1945—but not without writing his most famous comment, that it was New Zealand's destiny to have produced certain men: "Everything that was good from that small, remote country had gone into them—sunshine and strength, good sense, patience, the versatility of practical men." He pointed out in a remarkable little book, *Report on Experience,* that New Zealanders were a little uneasy around educated Englishmen, and "very defensive. New Zealanders never liked having their deficiencies pointed out to them." I hesitate to say it, but I must: I recommend that one needs to perform expert surgery to remove once and for all a congenital anatomical defect, namely a small white bone fragment (known medically as a chip) on the upper torso (the shoulder). (The Irish comedian Dave Allen, when he visited New Zealand in 1978, quipped: "New Zealanders are the most balanced people in the world— they have a chip on each shoulder.") Along these lines, would it not be a good idea to let those tall poppies grow to their natural height, and refrain from treating them as weeds that require removal? Remove "tall poppy syndrome" from the list of dangerous diseases and embrace what stands out. Admire what is unique and exceptional.

Many people consider New Zealand to be the Sweden of the Pacific. In some important ways, it has yet to earn this title: Sweden is a successful welfare state; they have serious farm animal reform bills in place, and they take children's rights very seriously (including the right never to be hit). These are still goals for New Zealand. It is much easier, of course, to be a physical paradise (which New Zealand is) than to earn the title in other ways. I do believe, however, that New Zealand is moving in the direction of a happy, healthy society, a multicultural society, and one that will hopefully one day be completely free of perhaps the greatest blights on our planet: racism, child poverty, and ethnocentrism. I am proud that soon I shall be a New Zealand citizen, and will be free to work for those goals in my very own country!

chapter 7

A Conversation with a Great Ordinary Kiwi: Sir Edmund Hillary

New Zealand's greatest icon lives in a modest bungalow on Remuera Road, in the heart of Auckland. I was bringing as a gift a load of books I had written, hoping to ingratiate myself and be able to spend with him more than the five minutes he had promised me. Lady Hillary, who met me at the door, told me that Sir Edmund, the great conqueror of Mount Everest, was resting for the moment. I did not realize that this was her polite way of saying he could not see me after all.

"No problem," I said obtusely, "I am happy to wait."

"It's not necessary, you can just leave the books with me."

I was crushed. I saw my hopes for a lively meeting go out the window of his modest little bungalow.

"Could I just see him for a few minutes?" I pleaded. "He asked me to come [let's call this an exaggeration] and wants to see me [a blatant lie]."

My face had fallen so far she must have taken pity on me.

"Just a few minutes, though, he tires easily," she said, relenting. She saw one of the books I had brought, *The Nine Emotional Lives of Cats,* and brightened. "Are you fond of cats?"

At that moment her handsome ginger cat appeared, and he answered for me, winding himself against my leg and speaking to me.

"He speaks?"

"He has a lot to tell. He disappeared for four days. We heard a constant meow above our heads and assumed we were missing him so much we had started to hallucinate. Eventually we realized that he was trapped between the ceiling and the roof. He can't stop narrating his adventure!"

Sir Edmund Hillary appeared as she was telling me this story, and Lady Hillary left us alone. He was a craggy man, with bushy eyebrows, white sideburns, and long wild hair, considerably smaller than I had expected (the ravages of age—after all, he was eighty-four years old). He was armed with a beaming smile on his face (revealing somewhat damaged teeth—not one to consider appearances, he never bothered with dental care). He seemed genuinely happy to meet a complete stranger, as if he were looking forward to a good chat. There was no way he could have "put on" such a smile; here was a man who obviously liked people.

I handed him several books I had written, including *My Father's Guru.*

"This is my coming-of-age story about living with a pleasant fraud in Southern California. I thought it might interest you because I understand your father and mother were part of

'Radiant Living,' a kind of cult, wasn't it?" Sir Edmund looked a bit taken aback, as if he was so used to immediate questions about Everest that he did not expect other kinds of questions. He looked pleased.

"I haven't thought about that for a while. Well, it was not exactly a cult; more like a combination of Christianity, psychology, health, and physical fitness."

"So no fake cult-figure?" Sir Edmund seemed a bit surprised at how quickly we were entering deep water, but was not displeased.

"Not really, unless you consider Herbert Sutcliffe a guru. I suppose in a sense he was, or wanted to be one." (Later I learned that Sutcliffe, 1886–1971, was, just like my family's guru, very involved in diet, recommending fruits and vegetables before this was fashionable—and what is more unusual, he seems, like my father's guru, to have pretended to have a PhD when it is not likely that he ever obtained that degree. Sir Edmund was briefly his assistant, just as I was groomed to be the successor to our family guru.)

"Well, the man who was my father's guru, an English journalist by the name of Paul Brunton, who introduced Indian spirituality to the West in the 1940s, was not really a cult-figure then, though he was to become one. Nor was he really a nasty fraud. He was not particularly charming, but he was benign. He meant well."

"In what way was he a fraud, then?" Sir Edmund wanted to know.

"Well, for example, when I commented that I was surprised that he never learned to drive a car, he told me: 'You see, Jeffrey, on Venus, there are no cars,' as an explanation. I was meant to understand that he came from a different planet. I was eight when he first told me this, and my own reaction was 'Wow!' Later I considered it a delusion, though one that did not seem to affect his ability to live in the world in a more or less normal way."

I had been forewarned that Sir Edmund was tired of talking about Everest and The Summit and he did indeed seem glad we were talking about something else.

"Another thing, Sir Edmund," I began, when I was interrupted:

"Just call me Ed." There it was, my first taste of his almost pathological modesty. *I'm just a rough old New Zealander* is his refrain.

"Okay, Ed, thank you. The man I describe in this book, the actual guru of my father, Paul Brunton, whom we called P. B., took a great interest in other so-called spiritual leaders. When I was young, he told me to read Alexandra David-Neel's books about Tibet. So I read *Magic and Mystery in Tibet, Initiation and Initiates in Tibet,* and *My Journey to Lhasa,* all written in the late 1920s."

"Yes," he said enthusiastically, "I read them, too. They fired me up!" He was clearly happy to have found somebody else who knew about the strange and fascinating Alexandra David-Neel.

"Me, too. I believed every word of them then. I was too young for skepticism, though I think she really was the first foreign woman to reach Lhasa [disguised as a Buddhist monk] in 1924. It took her three years of travel to get there, though."

"I believe it is true."

"That could be, but I still think she was a very charming fraud. P. B. sent us to meet her in her country house in the south of France, in Digne, in 1957. I was sixteen at the time, and she was born in 1868, so she was eighty-nine. Completely remarkable lady, even then, full of fun and mischief. I believe she applied for a passport renewal when she was one hundred and got it! She wanted to continue traveling. She got on very well with my father, who was French and who also loved to travel. He always said that restlessness was in his blood, and he might be right, because I seem to have inherited the trait as well. She definitely had that same itch, to a quite extraordinary degree. She lived in what was then called Ceylon, and India, and China, and Mongolia, long before anyone else had thought of going there."

"Why do you say she was a fraud, then?"

"Because much of what she recounted to us and in her books simply could not be true. She was, though, quite a character. I was completely fascinated by her and asked her whether the 'stories' she told in her books were true. 'Oh yes,' she said, 'completely true.' 'You mean, even that story about the Tulpa, the phantom monk? You really just created him out of your own concentration?' 'Definitely true,' she insisted. 'In fact, at first he was very pleasant, a fat, jolly sort of man. But he changed; he became lean and mean, a truly sinister character. I was not the only one who saw him; everybody was afraid of him. I was, too, and I hated him. He began making sexual advances. Do you know what that is?' (I was embarrassed, because I wasn't sure, but I said I did.) 'I had to dissolve him, to evaporate him, and it was not easy, let me tell you.' Her eyes were sparkling and she had a teasing look. My father and P. B. had a long dissection of this interview and decided that David-Neel had simply seduced a young, happy-go-lucky monk who later became emaciated from sheer exhaustion! The Tibetans, P. B. assured us, were very credulous of any claim concerning the supernatural, and this gave her great cover for her trysts. She probably tired of her poor lover and sent him packing."

I thought I had gone on a bit long and was afraid of losing Sir Edmund's interest. Anything but: "I am very interested in what you say about frauds, because, you know, the truth is, I consider myself a fraud," said Sir Edmund, to my great surprise.

"You?" I was genuinely taken aback. My five minutes were long up, but we were on a roll and for the next two hours nobody came to disturb us.

"Yes, oh, I don't mean in the way you have just described Paul Brunton or David-Neel, but in terms of how other people see me. There is such a gulf between who I know myself to be and the way others think of me."

"How so?"

"Well, they think I am a hero, a great man. And I *know* I am nothing of the kind. I am quite an ordinary man, just a normal person."

"Wait a minute," I protested, "you are the world's greatest explorer and mountain climber."

Sir Edmund waved his large hand as if to shake off what I had just said. "Nonsense, there are many climbers better than me. My friend Reinhold Messner, for example, is a much better climber than I am." Messner was the first person to climb Everest without supplemental oxygen, and solo, too. He is also the first person to climb the eight highest mountains in the world, mostly solo.

"Well, maybe, but you are eighty-four and he is twenty-four years younger than you. But in 1953? If there were better climbers then, so much better than you, why didn't *they* climb Everest? It wasn't as if nobody tried, right?"

"You have a point," he reluctantly conceded.

"You couldn't have been just an ordinary climber, either."

"No, actually I wasn't. I was strong and I was very fast. And I was determined. I always had that. Oh, and I was confident. I knew I could do things. I hated to quit. And I had a great partner."

"You mean Tenzing Norgay?"

"Yes. He was the only Sherpa I knew at the time [today it is different] who absolutely longed to get to the top. It wasn't just a job for him; it consumed him."

Maybe Sir Edmund did not normally like to talk about Everest, but it seemed now he wanted to. Perhaps it was the slightly odd angle at which we were coming at it.

"Why did he want to get there so badly?"

"What do you mean why?"

"I mean, did you ever ask him why he wanted that?"

"No, actually I never did." Sir Edmund was pensive a moment, and I wanted to push him on this, but it felt, well, pushy, so I didn't. Tenzing, as a very young man, had previously been on a 1936 British expedition that was defeated by an early monsoon. In 1952 the great Swiss climber Raymond Lambert had chosen Tenzing to be his partner, and they had reached the South East Ridge, within sight of the summit.

"You know, when we got there, the very first thing he did was to dig a small hole and bury some good Swiss chocolate for his deities. He was a very pious Buddhist."

"And you? What was the first thing you did?"

"Well, we were only up there for ten or fifteen minutes, but when I saw him do that, it jogged my memory. You see, John Hunt, the leader of our expedition, had asked me a few days earlier if I could do him a favor. He was a lovely man, and I could never have refused him anything. 'Ed,' he said in his very English way"—and here Sir Edmund did a good imitation of a cultured colonel's English accent—" 'would you mind, should you happen to get to the top, would you mind awfully doing me a favor?' He said that a Catholic priest had given him a small plastic cross and asked that if he ever reached the summit of Everest, would he plant it there."

"So you said, 'No worries, mate!' Right?"

"Exactly!" Sir Edmund laughed with a booming voice. "Now, I'm not at all religious, but I do consider myself a reliable friend, so as soon as I remembered I took out the cross and dug a little hole and buried it. You know, later, a priest came to my door, and said that he had something for me. From . . . that guy in Rome, what's his name, you know, the head bloke?" Sir Edmund's memory may have been getting slowly weaker, but I was amazed at how the names of faraway villages and places still rolled off his tongue during our conversation: Phakding, Pangboche, Okhaldhunga, Duydh Kosi Valley, Namche Bazaar, the monastery of Thyangboche. These were as real to him as the suburbs around Auckland, Manukau, Mission Bay, Kohimarama, and Glendowie.

"You mean the pope?"

"Yeah, that's the guy. He had a medal from him to me for having placed the cross on the summit of Everest! I didn't tell him I buried it actually!"

"Is that all you did on the summit?"

"No, I looked around for Mallory. Even though I knew actually that he hadn't made it to the summit." George Mallory and Andrew Irvine were killed in 1924, close to the summit of Everest. It was unclear at that time if anybody could go higher than 24,600 feet and survive, or whether supplemental oxygen could help. An American team, the Nova expedition, with climbers Eric Simonson and Dave Hahn, found Mallory's remarkably well-preserved body in 1999, two thousand feet below the summit. It remains unclear whether he was ascending or descending when he fell and died. The Kodak camera he was carrying, which could well decide the question, has yet to be found.

"And then?" I asked.

"Well, here's the funny part. Remember a few minutes ago you told me that you were a restless man?" *My goodness, I thought, this great man is not just gracious, he actually listens to what people say to him.* "Well, that word doesn't even come close to what I feel."

"You are probably the originator of the American slang expression, *Been there, done that.*"

"Yes, precisely how I feel. *Next!* I want to shout. In fact, do you know that when I wrote my first book I wanted to call it *Battle Against Boredom*, but my publisher wouldn't let me. Anyway, I looked over at Mount Makalu; it had not yet been climbed, and I figured out a route in my mind to get to the top." Mount Makalu, in the Khumbu region on the Chinese–Nepalese border, just nine miles east of Everest, is the fifth highest peak in the world.

"Did you climb it later?"

"No, I never did. But I told the leader of a French expedition about the route I imagined, and he actually used that very route to get to the top."

"Do you think it is this determination to get places that singles you out?"

"No, actually, what I had, what I *still* have, is a rather rare ability to change my mind, to alter my plans."

"You mean if somebody tells you: 'Look, I have a better route,' you could graciously accept that he could be right, and give up your plan and substitute his plan?"

"Not graciously," he said, laughing, "but after making it my idea in the first place." My turn to laugh. "I would act on it if it was a better plan, yes, I definitely would. You see, I have a great passion to persist, I mean to live. So many great climbers die, and here I still am! I had had my share of accidents; I was buried in an avalanche, I fell down an ice crevasse, but I was always a careful climber, always very prepared."

"Were you and Tenzing similar?"

"As climbers, we were practically twins. He was much smaller than me, of course, but he reacted very quickly. There was a time when I jumped onto an ice ledge; it gave way, and I went straight down, plunging to the depths in this ice cave, as in an elevator."

"Did you think *That's it. Now I am going to die?*"

"No, I knew that Tenzing would do the right thing."

"But you are so much heavier than he is, didn't your weight just pull him down with you?"

"No, he planted his ice pick deep into the ice, quickly wrapped the rope around it as far as it would go, and of course it held. I was suddenly stopped, hit the side of the ice, and was able to pick my way to the top. He was good at this kind of thing, and so was I."

"So he was a good friend to you?"

"Oh yes, he was a close friend. His English was poor in 1953—an odd mixture of Hindi and English. But we seemed to understand each other easily." Sir Edmund seemed lost in thought for a moment. I hoped I was not bringing up difficult memories. He sighed, and continued: "But he led a sad life, and I could not seem to help him."

"How so?"

"Well, Nehru built him a kind of palace in Darjeeling. He sent his sons to be educated in America, and I think he felt lonely way up there, more or less isolated. He always thought that I had made better use of my time. He was happy that I was doing so much for the Sherpas, but he felt that he had failed them somehow. To some extent it was true."

"What happened?"

"Well, you know we were talking a few minutes ago about heroes, and how I don't feel like one. But there are some people who just seem made to fit that mold."

"Do you have heroes?"

"Oh yes, Shackleton, my friend Eric Shipton, and the Dalai Lama—who could resist his chuckle after all?" It was strange to think that the young Tenzing managed to get on Shipton's much earlier 1935 Everest expedition—he had been only nineteen at the time, and was newly married. Later, by the time Sir Edmund met him, Tenzing had spent more time on Everest than any man on earth.

"But that is not what I was going to say. I was going to talk about a man who had charisma, he really had it. (I met Bill Clinton, and he had it, too.) That was Pundit Nehru. Tenzing needed a passport to go with me to London, and the Nepali authorities were slow in responding. Nehru said, 'I will have one in a few hours'; he issued peremptory orders, and sure enough, later that afternoon a passport was brought, to everyone's amazement. Nobody disobeyed Nehru. He wanted to take Tenzing under his wing, to make him responsible for training

Indian climbers. Tenzing did not know how to say no. I think if Nehru had asked *me* to live in a palace in Darjeeling I could not have said no, either. He had that commanding personality. The entire Nehru clan came to visit him in Darjeeling, and there is a photo of Tenzing, Nehru, and three future prime ministers. Heady stuff, but probably not the best thing for Tenzing. In later years he drank too much, and died relatively young, in 1986 I believe—he was just seventy-two."

"What did he die of, then?"

"I would have to say of a broken heart," Sir Edmund said sadly. "He would say to me—you know, once his English got better, we talked a lot—'Ed, you do so much, and I do nothing.' It was not true, but I could see it from his point of view. It was not jealousy, it was some sense that he was letting down his own people."

"You know, when you said that Eric Shipton was a hero for you, isn't it nonetheless true that even heroes can have feet of clay?" I am not sure what I was fishing for—perhaps a self-revelation? Shipton wasn't that much older than Sir Edmund, just eleven years. He, too, died young, before he was seventy.

"It seems to me that you are very interested in finding flaws in great men. Is that true?"

Touché. Sir Edmund had me!

"Yes, it's true actually. But look, it doesn't hurt to recognize somebody has a weakness; that doesn't mean you dismiss them totally."

Sir Edmund may have been kind to an extraordinary degree, but it did not mean he was without a certain sharp aware-ness. "Yes, I think I know what you mean," he admitted. "I adored Shipton, but he did have certain weaknesses."

"He believed in the Yeti, for example, didn't he?"

"Well, I don't know. He had the single best photograph of a Yeti footprint—or paw print, depending on what you believe."

"What do you believe?"

"Oh, there is no question of it. I saw that photograph and I thought even then, *Old Eric's up to something here.* He was not a dishonest man, but he loved to tease, and I am sure he just made a few improvements in the snow with his fingers!"

"So you think Messner is right, the Yeti is the Himalayan blue bear?"

"Unquestionably."

"Didn't you see some footprints on your way up Everest?"

"Yes, they were pretty high up, where you wouldn't expect any animal to go. But I noticed that these footprints looked very different in the sun and in the shade. It's like the sun has a distorting factor, and they appear huge, but when you see them in the shade, they look far more modest."

"Did you see any other animals that high up?"

"Just a lone Indian crow. He seemed to take pleasure in fol-lowing us almost to the top. Circling around—I think he was curious: *What on earth are they doing up here?* Birds must have thought it was ridiculous to climb to something they flew over so easily! But I want to come back to the Yeti for a moment. You know, I was commissioned to do a scientific expedition in 1960 by the Chicago *World Book Encyclopedia,* and among other

Mount Cook, South Island

Typical New Zealand scene, Hokianga, North Island

Ilan, Sofia, Manu, and Emile on our climbing tree at Karaka Bay, Auckland

A stream through
the native rainforest
in the Waitakere
Ranges, west of
Auckland

Jeff and Manu in
front of a waterfall
at Coromandel

Sunset in Karaka Bay, as seen from our home

Lake Tekapo, South Island

Bay at Coromandel Town

River near Queenstown, South Island

Six-hundred-year-old Kauri tree

Mount Taranaki, North Island

Lake and Mount Tarawera near Rotorua

Water garden
in Coromandel

Ilan and his friend Sofia in front of a typical Maori house in Rotorua

Marine reserve at Tawharanui, one of the most spectacular spots on the
North Island, near Warkworth

things (we were supposed to look at the effects of oxygen deprivation at high altitudes, and tried, unsuccessfully, to climb Mount Makalu), we were to settle the question of the Yeti. We found a skull, but no bones, just some old preserved skull-skin with a huge head of red hair. Villagers high up in the Himalayas told us this was definitely the Yeti. I took this to three different museums in the United States and London, and it was definitively identified as the hair of the Tibetan or Himalayan blue bear. Why the blue bear has red hair I don't know. It is a very elusive creature, and hardly anyone ever sees one. But the description and the behavior match. It can certainly kill a large yak with a single blow, something the Tibetans believe about the Yeti."

"Did Tenzing believe in the Yeti?"

"I never asked him, but I am sure he did. Everyone in Tibet does. But they never say exactly what it is. *Abominable*—that was just a phrase used by an American journalist. Sometimes they think it is benign and other times frightening. I am not even sure they think of it as supernatural at all. I wrote about this somewhere."

There was a pause in our talk, and Sir Edmund glanced through the books I had brought him. "By the way, thanks for all these books. I see you have written twenty books. Well, I haven't written that many, but I am very proud of my books. This house, modest as it is, was bought from the proceeds of my very first book." The rest of the proceeds from his many books were to go to various charities for Nepal. I don't believe anyone has ever accused Sir Edmund of greed. I wished to prolong our conversation, though, for I could see that he was not the least bit tired, and I knew that I would probably never get the opportunity again. So I questioned him again: "When you came back from Everest, how did your parents react?"

"Well, my dad was a very reticent individual, not very demonstrative, so he just said, 'Awh, good on you, mate.' My mother was much more excited, though."

"And what did you want to do when you got back?"

"Look after my bees!"

"And did you?"

"Yes, for a year, with my brother Rex, a builder and a bee-keeper. I loved beekeeping. But the demands on me got more and more frequent. I had become, without expecting it, a world figure. That is what I meant before by the difference be-tween how *I* saw myself and how others saw me. I was just a Kiwi beekeeper who had climbed a hill—okay, a mountain. No big deal. That is not how others saw it. But I soon realized that while the fame itself was always embarrassing to me, it could allow me to do some good for the world."

"Did you always feel that you wanted to do something use-ful in the world even when you were young?"

"Oh not at all." He laughed. "When I was very young, all I wanted to do was play with swords; then a bit later I wanted to rescue pretty girls, and then at sixteen I discovered mountains, and that was it."

"I can guess the answer to my next question: What is more important to you, climbing Everest or setting up schools and hospitals in Nepal?"

"You know the answer."

I did.

"Was Everest, though, your favorite adventure at least?"

"Not really. I most enjoyed going up the Ganges to find its source in the Himalayas. We went with boats, New Zealand jet boats, and I went with the world's best pilot, Jon Hamilton, the son of the man who invented these remarkable riverboats."

The boats had been invented in 1953, the same year Sir Edmund climbed Everest. I knew the boats. I told Sir Edmund that I saw them in Queenstown, and Ilan, who was six at the time, insisted on going on one with me. "To be honest, I was too frightened. They are so fast, and go so close to the cliffs that border the river. Ilan was disappointed in me. He will be glad to hear of your adventure, and I will start reading your account of jet boating up the Ganges, *From the Ocean to the Sky*. I have a copy here, and would be honored if you would sign it for me."

"Of course, and all the other books of mine I see you brought along."

"Thank you. What particularly did you like about that trip?"

"I loved seeing millions of happy people along the banks, cheering us on. It felt good to be among a friendly, gregarious people, instead of nearly alone on a cold mountain."

"I heard that when one of your friends, Jim Wilson, sank one of the boats, and he dreaded having to face you, you just laughed it off, gave him a bear hug, and said let's get on with it."

"True, why make a fuss over something that's done anyway? I was never one to obsess about the past. Too much to do in the future!"

"What about the polar expeditions?"

"Yes, I loved that, too. Did you ever read Apsley Cherry-Garrard's marvelous book, *The Worst Journey in the World?* It is my favorite travel book."

"I loved it, too. He was the only survivor of Scott's last journey to the South Pole in 1913, wasn't he?"

"Yes, well, I had always been fascinated by both poles. I was on the Commonwealth Trans-Antarctic Expedition led by the English explorer Vivian 'Bunny' Fuchs in 1955. I had been inspired by the Scott and Shackleton expeditions. My New Zealand team sailed there on the *Endeavor,* and we established Scott Base. I was supposed to make food depots from the Ross Sea to the South Pole, training dog teams for the job. I decided to add Ferguson farm tractors to the team. I grew up on a small farm in Tuakau, just south of Auckland, so I knew all about these wonderful machines. They could go anywhere, I knew that. I went to Norway and got them specially fitted out with large chains for the ice. In 1957 I actually made it to the South Pole before Fuchs, with the tractors! That was great fun, especially when they got stuck in a crevasse, and we would have to find a way to haul them out. The dogs thought we were crazy."

"Speaking of animals, I wrote a book about the amazing fathering ability of the emperor penguin. Did you ever see any of them down there?"

"Oh yes, all the time, everywhere. But you know, it is true, they are amazing fathers. They keep that egg on their foot for months while they fast and huddle from the cold. But they are also very stupid. I remember one time unhitching the dogs from the sledges, and they made an enormous racket, so relieved were they at being free. They barked and jumped and there was a large emperor penguin not far away, no more than a hundred meters from us, or less. He had his back to us."

"Didn't you fear that the dogs would attack him?"

"Oh no, we kept them on chains, but in any event, when you see one standing near you, it is like seeing a person; no dog would attack something that large. But the interesting thing that I could not explain is that that dumb bird would not so much as turn around to even look at us, or find out what all the fuss was about! He just stood there, supremely indifferent, with his back still turned to us. Well, maybe he had an egg on his foot!"

"Do you ever feel bored in Auckland, or find it too narrow, too confining?" I was projecting.

"You must be kidding! I love it here—I can be outdoors so much of the time, and besides, I am never here for long. I am always traveling; perhaps half of the year I travel, still, and I love it."

I was reluctant to leave, and clearly Sir Edmund was enjoying himself, too. "It's been fun for me to think about these things, and I haven't laughed so much in a long time," he told me. I could have stayed another five hours and never been bored, but it was not fair to keep a man his age so long; besides, the phone never stopped ringing the whole time I was there.

Everybody wants to see him. The demands on him are enormous. But at the door, I wanted to tell him that even though we had both acknowledged weakness in the notion of a "great man" I still felt that he had one quality that no other great man I had ever known had, and that was genuine humility. He had insisted, several times during our conversation, that he was not really different from anyone else. And I believe, just as a philosophical point, that that is true. We are all unique in our own way, and even the greatest minds are only good at certain things. For example, Einstein was no genius when it came to human relations: Look at the way he treated his first wife.

"Do you think having been born in New Zealand helped?" I asked. "After all, nobody in New Zealand likes a tall poppy. Egalitarianism is *the* ideal here. You seem to have imbibed it with your mother's milk."

"True, true, New Zealanders hate to brag, or hear others brag."

There was nothing fake about Sir Edmund's modesty. But he also had one quality that I had never before encountered in a man of his fame: He was genuinely interested in other people and their experiences. At eighty-four, coming to the end of a long and illustrious life, he nonetheless asked many questions about myself, my family, my wife, my children, my life, what I had done, what I had written. There was nothing formal about this; he was not just being polite; he was genuinely interested. It was a wonderful quality, and I told him so. He thought for a moment, and then he laughed.

"You know," he said with a grin, "that reminds me of a night when I was stuck in a tiny hotel in the middle of nowhere, with Neil Armstrong. There was nothing to do but talk, and talk he did. For eight straight hours. And in that entire time, he never asked me a single question! Oh well, I don't mind, I learned a great deal about the moon!"

With that he laughed, shook my hand warmly and firmly—he was still a bear of a man—and told me that he had had a great time, that it was fun, and I should call him for another meeting sometime. I hope I can muster the courage!

"*E*ver since I reached the summit of Mount Everest fifty years ago the media have classified me as a hero, but I have always recognized myself as a man of modest abilities," is how Sir Edmund Hillary begins the Fiftieth Anniversary Edition of *Our Ascent of Everest*. This is neither false humility nor a stance, as I saw for myself during the two hours I spent with him. He means every word of it. But while the words ring true, and are true, they are not his words alone—or rather, the phenomenon of which they speak, modesty on a scale not to be encountered in any other man of his stature, is the product of the basic culture of New Zealand. Sir Edmund Hillary knows he is like his fellow Kiwis because he meets them all the time: people who have a talent, who can do something extremely well, and think nothing of it.

chapter 8

Maori: The People, The Culture, The Language

Auckland, with a total population of 1,158,891 at the last available census (2001), is the largest Polynesian city in the world. (Remember that Maori are also Polynesian.) That is, there are more Polynesians living in Auckland (almost 30 percent if we add the Maori and the Pacific Islander populations together) than anywhere else in the world. In Auckland only 68.5 percent of the population is European, compared to 80 percent in the country as a whole. The Pacific Islands are the third most common birthplace for people living in Auckland, and Samoan is the second most commonly spoken language (4 percent) after English. Maori are 14.7 percent of the total population of New Zealand—nearly seven hundred thousand people—and Pacific Islanders are 6.6 percent.* But while many

*Here is the breakdown: Samoans: 115,000; Cook Islanders: 52,600; Tongans: 40,700; Niueans: 20,100 (only 8,000 people live in Niue itself); Fijians: 7,000; Tokelauans: 6,200 (only 1,500 residents live in Tokelau, a New Zealand territory north of Samoa); and Tuvaluans: 1,960.

Maori live outside of Auckland, very few Pacific Islanders do. (The vast majority live on the North Island, and even there, most live in Auckland.) Their cultures add color and life to New Zealand. The city and the country would be a poorer place without them.

I love to hear the Maori language (closely related to Hawaiian and Tahitian) on the radio; it is a beautiful, melodious language, the Italian of the Pacific. Very few Pakeha—New Zealanders of European descent—speak Maori, or bother to learn it, sadly. Since it is, along with English, the official language of New Zealand, I cannot understand why it is not obligatory in every school in the country. You can, after all, demand that in a New Zealand court of law you be addressed in Maori. Fortunately, more and more Maori are learning the language early on, in the kohanga reo, the "language nests" begun in 1982. So successful have these efforts been that, right from the beginning, they served to inspire similar language nests, first in Hawaii, in Hawaiian, a cognate language, but also in other parts of the United States, in Native American languages. Recently Maori have started language classes for mothers with children sixteen to twenty-four months old, so that the babies can hear the sounds and rhythms of the language spoken around them while the mothers learn Maori at the same time.

I discovered when I asked Maori how to correctly pronounce a place-name in Maori that they were always happy I asked, and delighted to tell me the correct pronunciation. There is absolutely no excuse for not pronouncing Maori words and place-names correctly. The National Radio insists that all Maori words be pronounced according to Maori standards, not their anglicized equivalent. Everyone should follow this example.

*H*ow can I, a foreigner, write anything useful or fair or informative about the Maori? It is a question that has been asked of people far more knowledgeable than I, and the results have not been good. Michael King, for example, who has published dozens of books about historical issues concerning Maori, who knows the language and the traditions, has gone on record to say that he will no longer write about Maori issues. Attempting to help Europeans understand Maori values, quite successfully, it would seem, he said, "It never occurred to me that to do so might be considered inappropriate, nor that my presence in this role might eventually be unwelcome." Evidently a substantial number of prominent and intelligent Maori have asked him not to speak for them. They feel they can deal with their own history, and can give a better insider account than can anyone from the outside. He saw it "as a beginning to redress, in a small way, 150 years of Pakeha hostility or indifference to Maori things." It is obviously true that somebody from within the tradition would see it differently, but is it always a good thing to have nothing but insider accounts? I think not. Diversity is surely a preference. But perhaps I only think that because I have often been an outsider in what I have chosen to write about.

"How dare you write about Maori?" said a radical Maori activist who came down to Karaka Bay to visit me at my home on "her" beach—hers, even though she had never been there before. She was pleasant enough, but quite explicit: *her* tribe, *her* iwi, owned this land—I was trespassing. I got her point. "At least, though," she conceded, "you are enjoying it, not using it for commercial profit." I could see that I, too, would be upset if some foreign developer (actually, *any* developer) came along and bought up this beach to raise a high-rise apartment so expensive that only retired rich people from other countries could afford to stay here and that only for the warm months of the year. And yet, her iwi does not own the beach either. Nobody can own a beach.

When we visited Ayers Rock, otherwise known as Uluru, in the Northern Territory, some 280 miles southwest of Alice Springs in Australia, I was simply unprepared, as is everyone, for the effect this remarkable stone mountain would have on me. More than a thousand feet tall and nearly six miles around, this red sandstone is the world's largest monolith. The word *awe* seems purpose-made just for Uluru. Nobody owns that rock, of course. But the Aboriginal Anangu tribes of the Western Desert, who have been in the area for perhaps forty thousand years, feel a certain—what exactly is the right word here?—relation, perhaps, to that rock that somebody like me, who whizzes in and whizzes out a day later, cannot possibly have. I understand that. Nor do the local Aborigines claim to "own" the rock. They call themselves guardians of the rock, and they have put up the sweetest, kindest note at the base of the rock, urging "us" not to climb it because it is sacred to them. The note states that they cannot forbid us to do so, but they would be deeply grateful if we could recognize and respect their feelings in this matter. It was shocking for me to see tourists stop, read the sign, then continue the climb up the rock without the slightest hesitation.

Of course it helps that the Maori do not believe in *individual* ownership. It is not one person, but the entire iwi that owns land (and the phrase *to own* seems absent from the Maori language!). That is, the purpose of the land is one that must benefit the entire tribe, not just one or some individuals in that tribe. This is not to say that ancient Maori society was democratic: It was anything but. There was a rigid hierarchy, most notably between the few rangatiras, "aristocrats," and everyone else, the many commoners. Below the commoners came slaves, that is, women and children captured in war. But just as we must not compare "slavery" in animal societies (such as ants) with human slavery, nor should we think that all slavery was the same. After a period, some Maori slaves taken in war would marry into the tribe they were captured by, achieving "citizenship" as it were. The child of any slave was born a free person, a situation far different from North American slavery, a much more pernicious institution. Nor is it entirely clear whether rank was strictly inherited, or could be reached through achievements of various kinds, including knowledge. After all, a wise man, a kaumatua, is often simply an older person, and a tohunga is rarely born into that status; it is *acquired*. While in theory women were not supposed to occupy positions of rank and influence, in fact they often did.

The Maori activist's people had been here far longer than I

had, far longer than anyone I knew, in fact. New Zealanders like to point out that the Maori came just eight hundred years ago, and Europeans two hundred. Just? I might feel differently about this bay and this land if my ancestors had been here for almost a thousand years. So I understood her feelings. Even if this was her first visit, which it was. But this was only the beginning of our difficulties. Not at a personal level—she was most pleasant, a beautiful woman at fifty who had eight children and was accomplished in many areas. She was not eager, I could see, to tell me *anything*.

Soon it became clear that knowledge in Maori tradition is quite different from knowledge for me. My knowledge, almost all that I possess, is knowledge I have derived from reading. I read a great deal, in various fields. I have learned much. But this is mostly just book knowledge. I lack the feeling of knowledge intimately held, acquired with difficulty, against great odds, or achieved slowly over long times. Still, I have an insatiable curiosity. "Tell me," I asked her, "why do the Maori say that eels are the progeny of supernatural beings?" It is something I have always wanted to ask somebody well versed in Maori tradition. It had not occurred to me that I would not get an answer (which I did not); that the answer was not freely available for everyone. Maybe that is why I could not find it written down in any book. I did not understand, and still find the concept difficult to digest, that knowledge in many oral traditions is sacred—but its revelation can be dangerous. I suppose I was used to the tradition of ancient India, where knowledge, while sacred, was also meant to be handed down, and traditional Sanskrit Pundits loved that I spoke their ancient language and was curious about their texts. Most Pundits could not get enough of my questions and would speak with me in Sanskrit for as long as I could stay awake! The Maori tradition is different because it contains an idea foreign to the Indian tradition, namely that giving out information is dangerous to the person dispensing it. One traditional Maori, John Rangihau of Tuhoe, told Michael King that some older Maori believe that the knowledge they have is "part of their own life-force, and when they start shedding this they are giving away themselves." A person, he explained, could be left an "empty hulk" and "without purpose." "And it can create chinks in the armor of personal tapu ("taboo," because sacred), leaving a man vulnerable to physical and mental illness. It can even bring about death." No wonder many Maori are reluctant to talk with me; I ask incessant questions; bad manners at best, a critical danger at worst.

*T*he Maori told stories, composed poetry, made up lyrics, and did all the things any other civilization does, except that it was exclusively an oral tradition. Until recently. *How* recently becomes clear when one considers that Patricia Grace's *Waiariki* was the first collection of stories by a Maori woman to be published. When? In 1975! Witi Ihimaera, the author of the book (written in New York, when he was the New Zealand consul) upon which the phenomenally successful film *Whale Rider* was based (a film loved by everyone, including the Maori whose magical story it tells), is the first Maori to have written a series of short stories and published a novel, again only in the 1970s. The collection of other Maori authors that he edited in 1982, *Into the World of Light,* showed that the reason for this absence of published work has nothing to do with an absence of talent. Either the Maori, belonging to an oral tradition, were hesitant to set down their stories in written form, or a still-prejudiced public was not willing to read them. The Maori, from their earliest contacts with Europeans, recognized the value of learning to read and write, and quickly mastered both.

Maggie Papakura (also known as Makereti), a Maori woman born in Rotorua in 1872, went to Oxford in the 1920s to study anthropology. Her thesis about Maori customs, *The Old-Time Maori,* the first comprehensive ethnology written by a Maori, was left nearly complete at her death in 1930. It was published in 1938. But Makereti left instructions to check the appropriateness of the material with elders of her iwi, Te Arawa. Knowledge must be earned, not casually dipped into. What makes you worthy of this knowledge? How would you use it? Why should it be entrusted to you? How could others know you would not misuse it, misstate it, misunderstand it? Well, they could not. Once something was put down in a book, control was lost over how the knowledge was used. It was something of a matter of pride to Westerners that *anybody* could access what we had so painfully acquired. We rejoiced in its wide diffusion.

The difficulties compounded. To make myself more sympathetic, I said I was deeply impressed with how differently Maori were treated here than how the Aborigines were treated in Australia. "What bullshit!" my Maori guest replied. "Does that make what we suffer, the indignities, the injustice, any the less? The fact that we live less long, are more likely to be found in prisons, are on the average poorer than white people in this country—does this matter *less* because Aborigines in Australia are even *less* well off?" I had no ready answer for that, to be sure. I did not mean to minimize the situation here, but I could see how making the statement I just made inevitably meant that. My visitor had a good point.

I have said that sometimes I can become too PC for my own good. My belief about cannibalism is a good example. I read the anthropologist W. Arens's 1979 book, *The Man-Eating Myth: Anthropology and Anthropophagy,* and was convinced. Echoing E. E. Evans-Pritchard ("Both Europeans and Arabs seem to have a morbid interest in cannibalism and tend to accept almost any tale told them about it"), there are, he said, no eyewitness accounts of cannibalism, only second- or third-hand reports, so it seems it is something that people say about their enemies, to show their savagery, but never about their own culture. But I was wrong. I asked Anne Salmond about it, probably the world's leading expert on early Maori contacts with Europeans, and she said there was absolutely no doubt that the custom had existed among Maori. Since asking her, I have made a point of looking for it, and sure enough, there they were, eyewitness accounts. One account is by Augustus Earle (1793–1838), who stayed for eight months in the Bay of Islands, on the North Island, in 1827. He was present when a young girl, a slave who ran away from her master, was caught, and as punishment was cruelly killed; then her body was prepared for eating. Earle had been skeptical of accounts of flesh eating until the moment he actually witnessed it. The account is found in *The Writing of New Zealand.*

Joseph Banks, who was on Captain Cook's boat as the naturalist, described an encounter he had on January 16, 1770: "On asking the people what bones they were, they answered: 'The bones of a man.'—'And have you eaten the flesh?'— 'Yes.'—'Why did you not eat the woman we saw to-day in the water?'—'She was our relation.' 'Whom, then, do you eat?'— 'Those who are killed in war.' " Still, it is one thing to say it existed, another to understand it and explain the values behind it. Moreover, remember that we are talking about something that happened more than two hundred years ago. Imagine if American culture were judged or interpreted in the light of what happened in Salem!

When it comes to values, however, people point to the fact that Maori were fighting men, that it is a fighting culture. They say: *Aha, there you have it, see? Maori culture glorifies violence.* And Western culture does not? The Greeks? The Germans in the Second World War? The Americans today? *We* have no culture of violence? *Yes, but we also have a Western tradition of pacifism.* So has Maori culture. One film (*Once Were Warriors*) does not a culture make! *But you cannot deny that the Maori hit their children more than do Pakeha.* Actually, from 1990 through 1999, eighty-seven children under the age of fourteen were victims of homicide in New Zealand: forty-one were Maori, thirty-five were Pakeha, three Asian, two Indian, two Samoan, and four other. *Maori culture condones, even encourages violence against children, does it not?* What, exactly, is meant by *Maori culture* here? The Maori oral tradition? Certain cultural clichés that we hear over and over without ever seeing evidence for them? Our own limited knowledge of another culture? Moreover, are we talking about attitudes of five hundred years ago, two hundred years ago, one hundred years ago, or today? In fact, a recent survey shows that cultural differences are minor: Only a slightly higher percentage of Maori and Pacific Island families than Pakeha families endorsed physical punishment. And only a relatively small percentage of *all* people in New Zealand (12 percent) believe that hitting children is not justified at all. What matters are personal beliefs and personal attitudes and experience, not cultural affiliation. After all, who could say what the Western tradition toward children is? If we look at the past, as, for example, by looking at back issues of *The History of Childhood Quarterly* (or Lloyd de Mause's 1975 book *The History of Childhood*), we see a dismal, violent record, one that includes every possible form of torture, beating, and death of children from biblical times until today, in all Western societies bar none.

Something we must always bear in mind is that any account of child abuse, no matter how rewarded, or how authoritative the speaker, is only one view. I was appalled, I confess, at the depiction of murderous child abuse in the prizewinning novel *The Bone People* by Keri Hulme. To me, she seemed to excuse, justify, and finally forgive the violence to a mute seven-year-old boy. But this was a novel by one specific author. The fact that she identifies as Maori does not make her description either accepted by other Maori or an account of what Maori do or did in the past. It is one person's rather intellectually eccentric vision of child abuse within Maori culture. There is no way it can be said to represent anything. Keri Hulme is not writing an essay about child abuse here; nonetheless, her attitudes do come forth very strongly. She explains and more or less justifies the almost deadly beating that her main character Joe gives to the little boy Simon, at the definite instigation of the main female character Kerwin. She explicitly does this within the novel, suddenly dropping the unusually poetic language to give a straightforward excuse for the beating, one that could be provided to a defense lawyer. (Joe is given three months' jail time, while the child is in the hospital for a much longer period, most of it spent in a coma that doctors believe he cannot survive.) The important point is to realize that after reading this novel, you emphatically do *not* know about Maori attitudes about the physical punishment of children; you only know about Keri Hulme's fictional portrayal.

We must distinguish between violence toward children, which has only in very recent times come to be seen as a sign of psychopathology in the West, and society-sanctioned violence (in almost all cultures that have ever existed). The Maori did not consider violence to children acceptable at all. Consider the authoritative words of Makereti in *The Old-Time Maori:* "The Maori never beat their children, but were always kind to them, and this seemed to strengthen the bond of affection which remains among Maori throughout life." Now, this may be an idealized view, but it is an ideal shared by the culture as a whole, so that when somebody deviates from this ideal (which is frequent in all cultures) it would have been perceived as a deviance.

What is true, however, is that Maori culture, like most other world cultures, was very pro-war. We see this in the fact that the same book, *The Old-Time Maori*, devotes as many pages to a discussion of weapons as it does to children! The author writes: "War was looked on by the old Maori as one of the most important things in his life, and every man was born to it and brought up to it. There was no asking, or making a man go to fight. Every Maori man was a warrior." To demonstrate this, Makereti tells a frightening story: "Our ancestor Rangitihi, when leading a war party in battle had his head split open with an axe." He then used a climbing plant stalk to bind up his split head, and fought on, both macabre and considered heroic. It is this warrior culture that is now at cross-purposes with the modern world, no matter how congruent it was in earlier days. Sociobiologists argue that men have evolved to fight. This may be true, but society no longer rewards warriors in the way it used to, so that the skills needed (aggression, boasting, anger) are now considered counterproductive, except in times of war. American soldiers who returned from Vietnam learned to their despair that society did not value what they had learned and what they practiced there. They were misfits in a society that was slowly weaning itself away from war. I suspect the same is true of many young Maori men today, who wind up joining gangs like the Mongrel Mob and feeling they have found a community.

I thought a bit more deeply about being Maori in a culture where Maori values are so little understood. Can these values be respected? Can we admire something we do not really understand? I am reminded of the great aphorism by François de La Rochefoucauld (1613–80): "We do not admire what we do not understand." Think about it: Universities in New Zealand have had departments of American studies before they had departments of Maori studies.

We need constantly to bear in mind that our dominant culture has never been under any kind of threat of destruction, whereas Maori culture and even the very survival of the Maori people "have been under threat of slow annihilation since 1840" as Michael King explains. He thinks that Maori race, culture, and language survived because Maori eventually acquired immunity to diseases brought to them from abroad, and because they developed a "cultural immunity to the assumptions of European superiority."

One quite extraordinary fact about the Maori is how easily and comfortably they accept you as being Maori even if by other stricter definitions you could hardly lay claim to it. Just about anybody who claims to be part, any part, Maori, and *feels* Maori, *is* Maori. Thus Keri Hulme, who was awarded the Booker Prize in 1985 for *The Bone People,* said: "It's very strange, but whereas by blood, flesh and inheritance, I am but an eighth

Maori, by heart, spirit and inclination, I feel all Maori." No Maori would deny her this right. A neighbor who is only one-sixteenth Maori considers himself, and is considered by relatives, to be completely Maori.

It is difficult for us to accept that any traditional people could have been as blind as we are to the depredation of the environment. Surely they practiced care of their environment because they must have recognized that their very existence depended on wise use, on sustainable use. Not so, it would seem. The Europeans would no doubt have exterminated the moa, had the Maori not gotten there first. The difference is that evidently the Maori learned from this. At some point *after* the killing of the last moa, the Maori instituted the concept of rahui, originally to mean a mark to warn people against trespassing, but also used to mean a ban in order to protect a tree, a bird, or a fish from overhunting. (Maori also realized, long before any Westerner had, the dangers of erosion, and had terraced the hills to prevent slipping—see the fine book *Fragile Eden* by Robin Hanbury-Tenison for more about this.) Andrew Mitchell, in *A Fragile Paradise: Nature and Man in the Pacific*, writes about the early settlers in New Zealand, "The Polynesians had unintentionally embarked upon a gigantic ecological experiment, and its consequences were to be disastrous for the natural life-support systems of the islands, endangering the precious resources upon which the immigrants themselves depended."

Of course the Maori had a different, and deeper relationship to trees, than we, on the average, do today. They gave individual names to imposing trees. But originally, the first inhabitants of New Zealand, in their eagerness to eat the moa, burned down the forest that provided them with protection (they also wanted to plant domestic crops there). They were, as the evocative phrase has it, eating their own future. At least they had the sense to recognize this fact hundreds of years before any Westerner did. To have any kind of spiritual connection (i.e., to recognize a spirit in a rock, tree, plant, or animal) with your environment, as the Maori clearly did early on, is the beginning of ecological wisdom.

We like to make fun of the politically correct attitude of ascribing ecological wisdom to ancient cultures by displaying the sad lack of same in some cases, as we have just seen. Nonetheless there can be no doubt that the Maori, for whatever reason, had a much closer association with their natural world than did almost any Westerner until recently. Mountains, for example, in most Western art, were places of gloom and fear. Not so in Maori. When I was learning Maori (I did not, alas, get very far, but I have taken it up again with a native speaker), we were taught immediately how to introduce ourselves in Maori. We had to identify ourselves for an audience by reciting our whakapapa, "genealogy," but it had to include a mountain and a river that was of particular importance to our origin. Maori felt anchored to a particular place, a physical place in nature. Perhaps you remember that wonderful book that came out in 1974, by the legal expert Christopher Stone, with the astounding question in its title *Should Trees Have Standing?* Well, the question was a no-brainer for the Maori: Of course trees had standing. They even had names, individual names for individual trees of particular dignity, size, or historical importance. The Maori scholar Ranginui Walker says: "When I am in a forest I feel I am in the temple of Tane [the god of the forest]. For instance, one evening we went to see Tane Mahuta in the Waipoua forest. It was dark enough for owls to be flying around and yet that tree was bathed in an eerie light. I knew I was in a superior presence to myself." When he says this, he could be speaking for many Maori (and at least one non-Maori, me).

Nor does one associate the New Zealand landscape with the blood ritual of the royal hunt. Even for the Maori, hunting was not ritual but necessary to sustain life (so they believed, as did *all* hunter-gatherer societies). Nonetheless, the Maori observed taihuna, times when it was not permitted to kill animals. We assume, of course, that they did this because they were not ignorant when it came to ecological principles of replenishing game. It has never even been considered that perhaps they did it because they felt guilty about killing. Alas, no records—even oral, I believe—remain of the few vegetarian-minded Maori men and women from a thousand years ago.

chapter 9

A Very Personal Itinerary

Do you ever get the sense when you read certain guidebooks that the writer has not actually been there? Somebody has read the brochures, and made telephone calls, and perhaps called the tourist information bureau, but has not actually gone to the place to see what it's like. So here is an itinerary that I actually did take. It is not meant as a definitive guide, but as a personal selection of what I found most appealing about New Zealand. I found these places on my own, and there is nothing terribly esoteric about them; it is just that they are *not* necessarily the first things tourists do when they get here.

The North Island

I would suggest flying to Auckland, the one large city in New Zealand, and immediately renting a car. Being in New Zealand is a bit like being in California: You just can't see it without your own transportation. Remember that people drive on the left here. It is actually not all that difficult to get used to. (There is one exception: If you are about to make a left turn into a left-hand lane, you would assume that you have the right-of-way over somebody coming toward you who wants to make a right-hand turn into the same road and lane. Wrong. The person on your right *always* has the right-of-way, even when, as in this case, it is counterintuitive.) I must confess, though, that within an hour after arriving I found myself speeding along on a mountain road, bewildered to see a long line of cars coming toward me on my side of the road, the right! I had forgotten. Can you imagine what they would have said had you tried that in LA? Well, here they smiled and waved, and I never made that mistake again.

You must have a detailed and accurate map. Buy one right away at the airport and use it for every drive you take. I would go have breakfast or lunch right away in a suburb called Ponsonby. This is the "in" place—cutting-edge cafés serving soy cappuccinos, a good women's bookstore, trendy designer-clothes stores, lots of young people stylishly dressed; it may seem a little retro (almost as if they were trying too hard to be hip) to people arriving from Berkeley or Portland or New York, but it is the only place like it here. Moreover, it is easygoing and friendly, just like the rest of this little gem of a country. Next, go to Mount Eden, just a ten-minute drive from Ponsonby, and drive to the top of the volcano there, the highest spot in Auckland, for a gorgeous view. From the top you can orient yourself in the city, and it is worth looking around carefully, so that when you are driving you have some idea of which direction you find yourself in.

Then drive through the center of town, down to the Viaduct, the port where all the boats are, and after walking around for a short while, follow the coast (Tamaki Drive) going east. It is a lovely drive, and you will find yourself going through little seaside towns. (They are called villages here—and remember, a city is just a designation, not a place, so Waitakere City does not refer to an actual place, but to what we would call the county of Waitakere.) These towns are actually tiny suburbs of Auckland. The first one you come to is Mission Bay, which is a magnet to everyone, but especially to the foreign population in the city—you are likely to hear more foreign languages being spoken here than anywhere else. There is a nice beach, very usable in the summer (for swimming and sailing and kayaking), and seaside cafés, but don't tarry too long.

Continue following the coast, through Kohimarama, much smaller, and then St. Heliers, my own community, also on the ocean, also small (two streets), but remarkably friendly. My eighty-five-year-old mother lives here, too, and when the bank manager at ANZ (Australia New Zealand), Tony del Isole, comes out of his office to personally greet her, she is enchanted, and asks why we didn't kidnap her earlier to live in paradise. Follow Riddell Road along the sea until you come to Peacock Street and a sign telling you that Karaka Bay is at the end of the street. Park at the bottom of the street and take the steep path down to the beach, a five-minute walk through a stand of mature, magnificent pohutukawa trees. Stop along the way at a tiny, unpretentious monument, about three feet tall and derelict, that tells you the Treaty of Waitangi was

signed in this bay in 1842 by twelve Maori chiefs and a representative of the British Crown. When I asked Doug Armstrong, a city councilor and one of my neighbors, about this
benevolently neglected marker, he seemed puzzled that I
would expect anything grander. It is not in the New Zealand
character to make a fuss about anything, even the most significant document in their entire history! The beach itself is
where I live, halfway along the grass-bordered path right along
the sea, in the new house with all the books in it—that's me sitting on my deck reading and writing in the sun; just wave at
me, and I will wave back if you hold up this book.

You have now seen the best part of the coast around Auckland. If you are going to spend another day here, think about
taking a short ferry ride to Tiritiri Matangi, an island that is a
bird reserve; or if you love hiking, take the ferry to Rangitoto
(pop. 105) and climb this recent volcanic cone; or if you like
lost little islands with beautiful houses, go to Waiheke (pop.
8,000).

After lunch, I suggest you consult your map, get on the
Motorway and head north, past the city. When you see a sign
saying WESTERN MOTORWAY, 16, take it, and about four miles
along you will see an exit that says SCENIC ROUTE and indicates
the way to the Waitakere Ranges, the main forest area in Auckland. Follow the route to Titirangi. When you first arrive, you
will suddenly sense a difference in the flora: It is no wonder, for
you are now entering a genuine rain forest. I still find it odd
that there is a rain forest only half an hour's drive from the center of the city, with houses, lots of them, set right in the middle

of this amazing place of ferns and giant kauri trees. You immediately have the impression that you are going back, in botani-
cal terms at least, a million years. You are. How is it possible to
buy a house and have your backyard consist of these trees and
ferns and moss? I was so astonished when I first visited there
that I went straight to a real estate agent to ask about buying a
house, convinced that she would say: "What, are you nuts?
Can't you see that you are in the middle of a rain forest, one of
the few in the world still intact? And you want to buy a piece of
it? Give me a break." But no, she was polite and showed me a
number of homes, some quite lovely, all right in the middle of
this very rain forest, and none of them costing more than
$250,000 (that was three years ago, and prices have gone up
by about 40 percent since then; still, by world standards, an
amazing bargain, though a kind of sacrilege). I asked why
houses were so cheap there, still a lot cheaper, for example,
than in the middle of downtown Auckland, or even the very
suburbs you have just come from, Mount Eden, say, or Ponsonby, or St. Heliers or Mission Bay. Because, the agent explained to me, it is too far from the city center for many
people, and because it rains so much; after all, it *is* a rain forest.
Some people don't like that. I see the point, though on that
particular day there was brilliant sunshine and the charming
little village square once again seemed out of a movie scene. I
saw a road marked WAITAKERE SCENIC DRIVE (Route 24), and so I
took it, trusting that New Zealanders, who are known for un-
derstatement, really meant it, and I was not disappointed.
Great fern forests on your left, and the Waitakere Ranges on

your right, rising up to fifteen hundred feet, tree-clad bright green mountains as far as the eye can see, with, here and there, a little house tucked into the cliffs. Even though I have now taken the same drive dozens of times, I am still in awe of its beauty. It must rank as one of the great drives anywhere. I stopped the first time, and often still do, at the wonderful Arataki Visitor Centre, just some three miles out of the little town of Titirangi. I happened to arrive there when the architect who built it was there. When I introduced myself he promptly took me on his own personal tour of a building that is among the nicest visitor centers I have ever seen. It was full of information, too, about the 143 walks you can take in the ranges, and the animals and birds you will see. As you walk up the round pathway to the center, you will see many of the forest trees. Just across the street is a wonderful little one-mile walk, along charming pathways with trees marked along the way, where you get an even closer look at the vegetation. It is worth doing. Don't miss taking the little side trail that takes you to the kauri cathedral grove, an amazing sight.

Then I would suggest getting back in the car and continuing to the West Coast beaches, the wild, rugged coast of golden-black-sand beaches where *The Piano* was filmed (actually in Karekare), and go to Piha or just a bit farther north to Te Henga or Bethells Beach—desolate, often windswept, and dangerous to swim in. Then head back to Auckland.

Or, if you prefer not to drive out to what are called the Western Beaches, from Titirangi you can take the road that leads to Huia and the Whatipu Peninsula, the southernmost of the West Coast beaches. It is a mysterious drive, passing lovely hidden beaches on your left and rain forest on your right. When you get to Huia (consisting of just a few houses and a little store), you may feel you are in Hawaii. If you continue over the bridge into Little Huia, the unpaved road continues for some miles until it dead-ends at a meandering beach walk fringed with toetoe grasses (about half an hour, and you can easily go without shoes) that takes you to a wild beach. If you branch off from the parking lot to the right, you get to some deep caves near the ocean, including one called the Ballroom Cave, where there was a wooden dance floor in the 1920s. Highly recommended!

*T*he next day I suggest heading off to the Coromandel, a peninsula about a two-and-a-half-hour drive from Auckland. You take the Southern Motorway and get off at the turnoff past the Bombay Hills and Ramarama. (I find it endearing that Indians have moved into these areas, thinking they have something to do with India, which they don't; *Bombay* was the name of a boat, and *Ramarama* is not the Indian god-man Rama, but the Maori name of a native plant—*Lophomyrtus bullata*.) Follow the signs to the Coromandel Peninsula. Stop at Thames, the gateway to the Coromandel, which is just about an hour from Auckland, lying on the shallow Firth (a Scottish word, used of a narrow inlet of the sea) of Thames. It is a sweet little town where the river meets the sea, with simple little wooden houses in the hills above the one long road with shops, named for the English town of Thames, which it in no way resembles.

Have lunch at the vegetarian restaurant here, Café Sola, visit the gold-mining museum, walk along the boardwalk built through the mangrove forest, and then continue the delightful drive along the coast. The road is meant to be taken slowly—it is worth savoring and very narrow, so don't hurry. On the way, if you have the time, I suggest you turn off at the Tapu– Coroglen Road, which goes off into the hills on your right. If you have small children, stop on your left at the little animal farm (more a tourist attraction than a sanctuary, but charming). There are many birds and small animals of all kinds wandering around the handsome grounds. Continue a few more miles, and on your right you will see Rapaura Water Gardens, which has one of the most striking lily ponds I have ever seen. Wander around the magnificent gardens, then take the half-hour bush walk, and you will come to a series of waterfalls with little pools to wade in.

Back on the road, continue for about a mile, and on your left you will see parking for the SQUARE KAURI, which you reach by 150 steps on your right, going up the cliff. This is well worth the climb: It is a magnificent tree, some twelve hundred years old, about 150 feet tall, with a 30-foot waist! It is not clear why the loggers did not take it down. Did they feel appreciation for this godlike tree? Were they intimidated by it? For whatever reason, though they murdered many of the other ancient trees, they let this one stand, and it stands there still; majestic, imperial, a god. As you face the forest, across the road, you are looking out at the true native bush of the Coromandel Peninsula Forest Park. Even though only 3 percent of the ancient kauris are left, it is still a sensational view, with fern trees growing to enormous heights. In this native bush live frogs and New Zealand parrots. It is dense, more or less impenetrable, and best viewed from a distance. I would drive just another mile or so up the road, then turn back and continue on the coast road.

After about an hour of magnificent scenery, you will arrive in the quaint little Coromandel Town, which boomed once gold was discovered there in 1852. Now that the gold has disappeared, it has become a favorite tourist destination, both for foreigners and for New Zealanders. We fell under its spell immediately, and have wound up buying four acres on the river just outside of town, across the street from Driving Creek Railroad, a must-see. At 225 Driving Creek Road, you will see a colorful sign saying MANUMEA COTTAGES. That is what we own and rent. Kiwi Barry Brickell, a well-known potter, almost entirely by himself built this amazing little railroad that takes you through a rain forest. Along the way, he planted fourteen thousand native trees. Why did we fall in love with this place? Hard to describe, but easy to see. You will know why once you are here. Coromandel Town is considered almost a subtropical island. It is rich in Maori history, too. It is lush and friendly, and the local market carries four kinds of soy milk—my kind of store. Right next to the railroad is the vegetarian Driving Creek Café, one of the most delightfully casual cafés in all of New Zealand, run by an Israeli actor, Itai, where we had the best falafel in New Zealand. The little town is teeming with restaurants, and there are a seemingly endless number of places to stay, camping grounds, backpackers, motels, and bed-and-breakfasts. There is also a charming little gift shop called Weta Design with local arts and crafts and, most important, a Sivalinga (the god Siva, in India, has a mystic penis) rock with my name (literally) on it! Again, another example of Kiwi friendliness: I asked if this solid egglike rock was for sale, and the owner told me it was not, but I could have it as a present! I was touched, but embarrassed, and of course thanked her profusely, but declined. The next time I was there, I saw the very rock, with a tiny sign: JEFFREY MASSON'S ROCK. (Check it out when you come; it will probably still be there!) I would definitely spend the night in Coromandel Town.

There are so many wondrous walks and lovely drives nearby. Before setting off on the road back to Auckland the next day, go up the 309, a dirt road that follows the river, and stop at something called Waiau Waterworks, a splendid playground for children of all ages with the theme of machines that make water go around—great fun and ingenious (the word that keeps cropping up when you speak of Kiwi inventions, of which this is certainly one).

Go back via Whangapoua, on the other side of the mountain (take Route 25), and walk along the open-ocean beach there to the end, then continue walking along the rocks, cross over the small hill, and on the other side you will come to one of the most magnificent beaches you have ever seen, with the odd name of New Chums. (A new chum is somebody just off the boat to New Zealand—a settler, in the old days, who had just arrived.) It is a tropical half-moon beach, completely unspoiled, nothing but white sand and gentle blue ocean, and I guarantee you will be the only person there. For how many more years can there still be places like this? And why does everyone, me included, feel that it is a tragedy that the day will come when there are no such places left? As of this writing, I hear that the property has been bought up, the whole beach, by a developer. Shudder. A Hilton Hotel on New Chums, why is that such an awful thought? But it is.

Keep going south and you will come to what is known as Hot Water Beach (you will see signs directing you off to the left). This is actually one of the top tourist sites in New Zealand, though you would never know it. At low tide you can rent a shovel, dig a hole on the beach, and watch it fill with *hot* water from under the ocean hot springs! Careful, it can be almost boiling. Let it cool down and get in. If you have extra time, a marvelous forty-minute hike along the ridge to Cathedral Cove Marine Reserve in Hahei is good exercise and quite marvelous.

Back in the car, you are now going to make your way back to Auckland, driving through Whitianga. Just on the other side of town you will see a little sign saying WILDERLAND, one of the oldest hippie communities in this area, which was once chockablock with them. Now they sell organic produce. The owner, Dan, is in his late eighties, in a wheelchair, but he will probably be there, working his imaginative playground, including a tiny railroad that he built by himself, and which is heaven for children. He and the whole place represent some of the best of New Zealand character traits: independent, unpretentious, ingenious, sweet, friendly, a little bit lost, a hopeless economic prospect—and yet Dan has been doing this for the last fifty years.

You will continue on to Tairua, a featureless town in a beautiful spot: Stop for a good lunch at the Down Under. The owner is actually a vegan, but doesn't say so. Drive to Mount Paku, a few minutes out of town, and take the half-hour walk to the top for a spectacular view. Then get back in the car and don't stop again until you are in Auckland. Unless you are with kids: Then follow the signs that say BROKEN HILLS, and walk through the caves that were built as tunnels by the old gold diggers (see chapter 4), now filled with weta (the odd, ancient grasshopper-like insect peculiar to New Zealand). Your kids will talk about these strange insects for months, guaranteed!

A very short trip can be taken from Auckland on the Northern Motorway to Warkworth (on the way you can briefly stop at Puhoi, which was a "Dalmatian"—from the coast of Yugoslavia—village a hundred years ago), a small town with a fine secondhand-book store, about an hour's drive. Continue on the road until you see a sign that says TAWHARANUI REGIONAL PARK on your right. Go right to the end of the peninsula park, and take the one- to two-hour walk (depending on how enchanted you are) called the Eco Trail along beaches, up onto pasture, through native bush, and into a small but amazing puriri forest, before you come back in a circle to the beach itself, where you should plan to picnic and, if it is warm, swim. There is wonderful swimming here. If you take this trip early enough, or late enough, for lunch or dinner, continue on to Leigh and go for a good meal at the Sawmill Café.

Right outside Leigh you will see a sign pointing off to the right, to the Cape Rodney–Okakari Point Marine Reserve (where the University of Auckland conducts marine research), which is where you will find the tiny Goat Island just a few miles down the road. If you have snorkeling gear, here is the place to use it. You can also take a glass-bottom boat for an hour. Back on the road, if you can, continue on to Pakiri, which is a bit of a drive, but one of those amazing New Zealand beaches with white sand that stretches for miles, and of course there's not another single person in sight. If you feel like spending the night, there is a terrific bed-and-breakfast just away from the beach called Miller's Ark. They will serve you a delicious organic breakfast, most of it from their own garden, and then you can walk to the beach.

Another trip you can make from Auckland is to go north to the Hokianga, Maori country, which is very poor and very lovely, with hardly anyone there at all—certainly few tourists. You take a ferry at Rawene, which takes you across the bay; when you get there, turn left, and a few hundred feet up the road is the best backpacker we found in New Zealand. (A backpacker is a place where you rent an inexpensive room and share the kitchen, like a youth hostel.) At the "Tree House," say hi to Phil, a gentle Australian who knows immense amounts about birds. Enjoy his guinea fowl and tame white doves who fly about in the trees, and make sure you go on the short bush walk behind the cabins. The most holy place in New Zealand is not all that far away (it is a long drive, but entirely worth it): Point Reinga, the northernmost tip of the North Island, where the dead are said to leave for their journey to the sky. Along the way, we rented a bach on an exquisite beach, but I am not sure of its name. I think it was Pukenui. You will pass hundreds of little beaches on your way there or back, and can take your time exploring them. I am sure you will find one as lovely as the one we found. As you get close, you pass something called Ninety Mile Beach (which is not ninety miles long at all); people drive their cars along the stream down to the beach and then up the beach (at low tide)—not to be recommended. On the other hand, we walked along the stream down the beach, a long walk that I am not sure was such a good idea, since buses passed us, making me aware of the damage they were doing to the fragile riverbanks and sand dunes. I asked several drivers about this, but they seemed unconcerned or indifferent. When you get to the actual "point" at Point Reinga, you should walk to the end, for there you will see both the Tasman Sea and the Pacific Ocean, which meet there. Stretching below for miles are untouched sandy beaches (which, if you have the time, you can walk down to and stroll along).

Another short excursion you can take from Auckland in just a few hours is to visit the beach called Muriwai on the Western Motorway, which has a rare gannet colony along the sea cliffs—an easy, pleasant walk, and a must for any bird enthusiast. If you take this route, make sure you come back via the back road from Muriwai, which takes you through little farms in a charming valley. It's only about half an hour's drive.

I also recommend the drive to the heavily trafficked tourist city of Rotorua, known as "Sulphur City." Don't be put off by its reputation. For some reason, many New Zealanders despise Rotorua, perhaps because it has been a tourist attraction from early in the last century. It is a thermal hot spring city. As soon as you drive in, you notice something strange: Wherever you look, there is steam coming out of rocks, sidewalks, and gardens. Stop at the first park you come to and take a walk through it; you will see little ponds of bubbling mud, tiny geysers, little pools of boiling water. The smell of sulfur is everywhere, from hydrogen sulfide drifting up from natural vents that occur all over the city, in gardens, in backyards, even on sidewalks. Do visit the public baths, called the Polynesian Spa. We avoided the more touristy things to do (well, actually we were forced to take our children to the luge), but much loved the buried village, a Maori village just outside town that disappeared under the lava and ash when Mount Tarawera erupted in 1886, creating the Waimangu Thermal Valley. Four of these thermal areas are open to the public, and are quite amazing, well worth the visit. The largest and most spectacular is Whakarewarewa, but if you visit, you must walk with hundreds of other tourists. Waiotapu seemed less traveled, and really quite wonderful. Do not miss the opportunity to go to the island, Nokia, in the middle of Lake Rotura for a glorious hike to the top of this history-filled sacred spot. It may not be open much longer but for now you are allowed entrance.

There is another itinerary you can make from Auckland that includes the slightly more touristy Bay of Islands. I actually loved it. Probably the easiest way to get there is to come back via the eastern coast when you are in Cape Reinga, taking your time back. First you will come to the pleasant area around Kerikeri, with tons of vegetable stands, including organic ones, with good oranges and fruits; no need to stop in the town of Kerikeri, just continue on to Russell. This is a tiny, quaint little town on the ocean; once upon a time it was the capital of New Zealand. (Darwin visited it in 1832 and hated it; at the time it was full of criminals.) Very worthwhile is the boat tour that takes up most of the morning or afternoon. You stop at one of the islands and can have a marvelous hike or swim. We did both. Do not miss the Waitangi Museum, in Waitangi, just north of Paihia. We could easily have spent longer than the morning we were there. It is a superb historical museum that gives you a real taste for the Treaty of Waitangi, New Zealand's founding document. When you get back on the road, stop in Kawakawa to see the amazing toilets that the Austrian artist Hundertwasser designed and built; then at Hikurangi take the Marua Valley Road leading to the coast, which will take you to Woolleys Bay. As you meander along the shoreline, known as the Tutukaka coast, you will see a small parking spot for a lovely little beach called Whale Bay, half an hour's hike in. Farther along on the road you will reach Matapouri, which itself has a fine beach for walking.

The South Island

It is a bit of cheek for me to write about the South Island because I have only been there twice. But I loved every minute of the time I was there, and can't wait to return (especially to repeat the five-day bicycle tour through remote countryside that was magnificent). The South Island is just the way New Zealand must have been a hundred years ago. If you thought you were remote on the North Island, wait until you get south! The roads are fantastic, the people are unbelievably friendly and helpful, and driving is pure pleasure. Nothing is easier than to rent a car in Wellington, take the ferry over to the South Island, and begin a tour. Where should you go? Anywhere at all! You will soon find you discover your own little towns, your own routes. If you simply announce, as we did, that you want to drive around the South Island, a hundred helpful people will come scurrying over to give you, each one, a magnificent itinerary. You cannot go wrong.

What we did was to go down one side of the island, cross over at some point, and come back up the other side. You can do it either way. We took the West Coast road and came back along the East Coast. My one regret is that we got only as far south as Queenstown, and then drove to Dunedin to begin our journey back. (We had just two weeks to explore the island.) Here are some of the highlights of what we did:

From Picton, where the ferry lands, we drove to the glorious Marlborough Sounds, and spent the rest of the day swimming, walking, and kayaking. We spent the night there, then drove to Nelson. This is the major northernmost city of the South Island and is famous for being the sunniest spot in all of New Zealand. In the last year, property has boomed there; suddenly everyone (and that means lots of Americans) want to live there, especially on the coast. It is a friendly town (what town in New Zealand is not?), very relaxed (ditto), and a good place to stock up on everything for the long drive ahead. It is also the jumping-off place for one of New Zealand's great national parks, Abel Tasman National Park. The beaches there are good, but what we enjoyed most of all is the (busy) Abel Tasman Coastal Track (a hiking trail) around this huge park, of which we did only a few hours, since Ilan was only three at the time. You could make an excursion there that could last for five days. (Any guidebook will tell you more and give you good suggestions on how to do it, especially abbreviated versions.) You can take a boat from just about anywhere along the coast to see the small hidden bays; we did and highly recommend it. By the way, we camped just about everywhere. We found it was a fun way to get to know other families, and people are friendly at campgrounds. They are remarkably safe places, where nobody hesitates to leave their children at the playground while they wander about for a while. When we could not get space (not unusual in January, the height of summer) we stayed at backpackers, cheap, equally fun, and equally sociable, though you generally meet travelers from Europe rather than people from New Zealand. We spent the night in the tiny town of Kaiteriteri.

When we left the park, we came to the small town of Takaka and asked the first person we met on the street where we could get a vegetarian meal. He hugged us and told us we had come to the right place; in fact, we should unpack our car right now, and refuse to budge: "You have arrived in paradise," he told us. He had a point. He sent us to the Whole Meal Café, on Main Street, where we had a good meal and soon knew everyone eating in the restaurant. Of course, in a New Zealand town you never need to ask what street such places are on, because there is always only one street, Main Street—but Main Street bears no resemblance whatsoever to the American main street of a thousand cowboy movies. It is rather the complete mirror opposite: pleasant, easygoing, lacking in any sense of danger. A little boring, yes, but how nice to never fear a gun.

The population of Takaka could not be more than a thousand people, but the week we were there it was swollen by a dance festival, and it felt like we had taken the direct route, no stops, to America in the 1960s. Our newfound fast friend was wearing rainbow colors, but so was everyone else. Everybody we talked to seemed to want to hug us and invited us to stay forever in this little slice of hippie heaven, and believe me, we were actually tempted. *Alternative* is the word that comes easiest to mind—the air was redolent with the smell of hash—but then I found this word constantly coming to mind in lots of places we visited. It felt so unthreatening. Or maybe it was just that the whole of the South Island, in fact, the whole of New Zealand is an alternative to North America, a place where you stop watching your back and start watching the beauty of the place. We Americans have forgotten how intoxicating this feeling of being safe and among friends can be.

Just north of Takaka, along Highway 60, you will come to Pupu (or Waikoropupu) Springs, possibly the largest freshwater spring in the world (pumping out an amazing 317,000 gallons of crystal-clear water a day). Take the two-mile gravel road through the reserve; the scenery is stunning. There is a spot along the shore of the springs that, legend has it, contains a Taniwha (a Maori sea serpent). Ilan was determined to catch sight of him. And lo and behold, the water began to churn, and Ilan was sure he caught a glimpse of the Monster. Actually, the water at this spot is always bubbling and roiling, nobody knows why, and the claim is that right there is the deepest spot of the whole spring, so deep that nobody has ever reached the bottom. Intrepid scuba divers were in the ice-cold waters anyway while we were there, and just twenty-four feet down is one of the sources of the spring.

Back on the highway, continue along the edge of Golden Bay, along one of the loneliest roads in New Zealand (and there is plenty of competition), until you come to Farewell Spit, fifteen miles of sand dunes and one of the country's most important wading-bird habitats.

You have to backtrack, then, to get back on the road that will take you to the West Coast, also known as Westland. To be honest, I can't remember much of the trip between Westport and Greymouth, probably because I discovered to my dismay the one, the only, drawback in the whole of New Zealand outdoors: the formidable sand fly (they belong to the *Simuliidae* family, and are really blackflies). It doesn't sound like much—what could be so terrible about a fly who lives in the sand? Hah! This is a bloodthirsty, despicable creature, about the size of a flea, who bites (only the female does so) and leaves you feeling you will never stop itching. The minute it strikes, you know you have encountered an insect you did not know before, and you will begin a fast run back to the car. The Maori knew them as namu, and believe they were the creation of the goddess of death (sand flies also bite seals, bats, and birds, especially penguins). They are right. Take plenty of insect repellent and never leave the car without it, no matter how tempting that empty beach looks. In the South Island they are mainly on the West Coast and the Marlborough Sounds. They particularly like rain. Greymouth made no impression on me after this, except as the place where you can take (we did not) a train over Arthur's Pass and into Christchurch. Evidently, the scenery is magnificent.

We continued along the coast for an endless drive, broken only by an equally endless supply of signs that indicated walks of every possible length. We took the first and the second and the third, assuming they would be the last. There were hundreds, though, and judging from the quality of the half dozen we took, they are not to be missed. How can each and every walk in New Zealand be different from every other walk you have ever taken there? I don't know, but somehow it is. By the way, this area has the lowest population of any region in all New Zealand. You can sense that, too, because you rarely see a house, a dwelling, or even another car. And we were there in the height of the season. I can only imagine what it would be like to drive there off-peak. You will come to the colorful little town of Hokitika, famous mainly for its greenstone (New Zealand jade) and little stores—a great place to stock up on souvenirs to take home. We spent the night there. One thing

I regret we did not do—though we were correctly advised to do so—was get to Ross, and then take Highway 6 south along the northern edge of Okarito Lagoon to reach the breeding ground for New Zealand's only colony of kotuku, magnificent white herons, pure white birds with long necks. There are only one hundred of these huge, amazing birds left in New Zealand (though they are common in tropical Asia, Australia, and the South Pacific).

We came to the little town (more a gas station than a town) of Franz Josef, to see the glacier. We walked up to it, but I was a bad tourist, since I kept wondering out loud why we needed to see giant blocks of ice made of snow crystals. True, originally the glacier was shrinking, and then in 1980 it mysteriously reversed, but I kept grumbling "so what" to myself as I learned from placards these "interesting" facts about what looked like gray and dirty snow. Maybe, too, I had overdosed on ice when I lived in Switzerland, but I don't think I will ever miss the bracing cold of winter ice. New Zealand only has snow in the mountains, not in any of the major towns, even on the South Island.

For the next few hours we headed toward Wanaka via a mountain drive along lakes, forests, waterfalls, and gorges, and again we passed numerous well-marked short walks, all worth taking time over. Always you feel that here is scenery you have not encountered before, certainly not in Europe or North America. This is the advantage of driving through a country that was cut off from the rest of the world for millions of years.

Eventually, we arrived in Wanaka. Now, we were there

three years ago, and had no idea of what to expect. When we went to the local cinema, we were absolutely charmed by settling into an old car right in the theater, while other moviegoers sat on comfortable worn couches. The movie had a short break so we could all have ice cream that the owner had made just for the occasion. Of course we began to get to know the other people who were there. Where else can that happen? No, I mean it: Where else in the world will you sit in a movie theater and start chatting with everyone else there? Only in New Zealand. It is like life fifty years ago there, all the time.

Earlier in the day, as we arrived, we could see the Alps reflected in Lake Wanaka (whose depths actually go below sea level). We had a meal at an outdoor Japanese restaurant and played with the daughter of the Japanese owner, who told us he loved the town because he had never experienced racism there. Why didn't we, he suggested, think of buying a little place? Houses were not expensive. I wish we had. Prices since then have probably tripled, as other people, especially Americans, have found the charm of Wanaka, maybe because it is so close to Queenstown. Queenstown seems to be everybody's favorite town in New Zealand. It is not mine; but this may be simply because it reminds me of Tahoe or Las Vegas, though I admit the scenery is spectacular, the setting unique, the blue, crystal-clear lake (Wakatipu) gorgeous. Maybe I just don't like resorts, and this it certainly is. Mind you, if you like to bungee jump (it originated here), or take very fast jet boats at incredible speeds up a river, or ski in the winter, this is the place for you. The adventure capital of the world, it is called, with some

truth. The streets are always filled with people from everywhere, and there is a perpetual party atmosphere. And, like
everywhere else in New Zealand, it is completely unthreatening and remarkably friendly. No maître d' will ever snub you
here (or anywhere else in New Zealand for that matter). We
spent the night in Wanaka, which I vastly prefer to Queenstown, although Queenstown does have every possible hotel
and motel to choose from.

Here I must interrupt our itinerary to tell you that two
years after this first trip to the South Island, we took a five-day
bike trip from Clyde (not that far from Queenstown) to Ran-
furly. We never biked more than fifteen miles a day, giving ourselves plenty of time to enjoy every moment of the spectacular,
ever-changing scenery. Our path used to be an old railroad
track, but was dug up and turned into one of the great bike
routes anywhere, similar to a good gravel road. Of course serious bikers could do the whole route in a single day—but families with kids will enjoy the leisurely pace. It is called the Otago
Central Rail Trail, and can be walked, biked, or ridden on a
horse, in either direction. There are no cars, barely any hills
(just a few small ones), a trail, sixty-eight bridges, and the best
thing is that you get to see scenery you would not see from the
road, and every single mile it seems to change. It opened in
2000, and is one-of-a-kind in New Zealand (New York has
some, and we went on a shorter version of one in Cambridge).
We went with a group of friends, about ten of us, and stayed in
tiny towns, picnicked, stopped for walks and chats and just to
gaze in awe. I would gladly do this again, but I would wait until

Ilan was older. Manu was sixteen months old and happily en-sconced in the back of Leila's bike, but Ilan was six and very macho: "I can do anything you can do." He couldn't. Halfway through day one he went on strike and would not pedal an-other minute. This was New Zealand, so the problem was not serious: A cell phone away, the friendly store who rented us the bikes speedily drove out with an Allycat (like a tandem, ex-cept Ilan did not have to pedal when he did not feel like it), and he and I were able to ride together the rest of the trip. I still think biking is the best way to travel anywhere—you notice more, and you go at a speed that is still "human." I would say that humans evolved to ride the bicycle if I didn't know it is not a Paleolithic invention. It feels the most natural way to investi-gate new places. It is soothing unlike any other means of trans-portation, and I prefer it to walking, because it is just fast enough so you can never be bored. I hope I will still be biking at ninety!

We made our way to Dunedin, the second largest city in the South Island (which still makes it tiny by world stan-dards—less than 115,000 people). I could not warm to the city. It reminded me of a small town in Scotland (which I could not warm to, either—except for Edinburgh). Indeed, it reminds everyone of such towns, and is in fact built to Scottish specifi-cations for the mostly ethnically Scottish population. We ar-rived at five thirty in the evening, and it felt like the whole population had left after the announcement of an imminent nuclear strike. "Where are all the people?" asked Ilan, puzzled and slightly alarmed. We spent the night there, even though the hotels struck me as dreary as the town. We left the next day. But I am being unfair. Friends have since told me that the university (Otago) is one of the best in Australasia, and that students there love the town and the life, and remember it fondly into their old age. Actually, I did find, early the next morning, quite wonderful secondhand-book stores, and I am sure no place is as dreary as a tired family can find it on a rainy evening when they have no idea where to go or what to look for. We drove around the glorious Otago Peninsula, northeast of the city, the next day, and it was breathtaking; as beautiful as any place we had seen in New Zealand. We hoped to watch the yellow-eyed penguins return to their nests in Taiaroa Head, the northeastern tip, but were too early in the day for that. We did see the albatross colony, though, something I am glad I did not miss. We took a detour to see famous Mount Cook, and stayed at the modern lodge there, hiking into the mountains to see many tiny lakes. Well worth the trip.

We continued up the east coast, stopping at the spectacular Moeraki Boulders Scenic Reserve some twenty miles south of Oamaru. The huge, round, sixty-million-year-old boulders, some of which stick out of the cliffs as if they were being born from them, look like giant sea turtles that have washed up on the sand. It is a mysterious sight not to be missed. I felt the impulse to take one home. (They only weigh about fifteen thousand pounds each.) There were, surprisingly, only fifty of them, and it turns out that my fantasy was shared by many people: Thousands of much smaller boulders had been removed as souvenirs by tourists over the years, and only the largest immovable ones remain. They are what are known as "septarian concretions," that is, they were not formed by the sea, but by a chemical action of minerals within their core—adhering to a piece of shell, for example, and pushing their way out. Think of the grain of sand in the oyster that turns into a pearl.

We continued through the cute towns of Oamaru, and Timaru, and finally into Christchurch once again, a town that is far from my favorite, though it is the second largest city in New Zealand with almost four hundred thousand people. It is very English (much of the architecture is Gothic Revival, which I don't like), very Anglican, very flat (good for cycling), with good theater, an internationally respected university (Canterbury), the magnificent Arts Centre (where you can easily spend the day browsing galleries, shops, cafés), and good bookstores. Still, it just did not do it for me, maybe because small English towns seem to me best in England; here the ferns make them seem out of place. But as in Dunedin, I found the surrounding area magnificent, especially Banks Peninsula, and the little French town of Akaroa, famous for boats that will take you to see the world's smallest dolphin, the Hector's dolphin, found only on the New Zealand coast. I was in a minuscule bookstore there and saw the most beautiful white stone from the beach I have ever seen. I told the owner, and she handed it to me: "Here, it's yours." I treasure it to this day. It is situated on French Bay, named for a French whaling captain who "purchased" thousands of acres from a group of Maori in 1838 and intended to turn French all of New Zealand—but the

British sent a gunboat there to settle the matter in unfriendly terms.

We ended our tour in a rather unspectacular fashion by driving along the eastern coast through Kaikoura (good for whale-watching and nice places to spend the night) to Blenheim (forgettable) and back to Picton to take the ferry to Wellington for the return drive to Auckland. I regret, now, that when we were so close to the southernmost town in New Zealand, Invercargill (which has an old hippie, Tim Shadbolt, as mayor), we did not make the trip. It's not that I wanted to see the town itself, but the drive there is supposed to be beautiful, and you can then take a short boat ride to Stewart Island, the third largest island in New Zealand, population 450. I also hope one day to visit the unspoiled and mysterious Chatham Islands, the "last place on earth" (population less than 700), home of the Moriori, the subject of one of the most interesting books written about New Zealand (see my bibliography under Michael King). The Moriori fascinate me, because they were one of the few people to have completely renounced warfare as a means of settling differences. A most remarkable people. Seeing the island will be something to look forward to next year.

Well, there it is, a very personal itinerary. It is just a start, but not a bad one. There are literally thousands of places anyone can discover by simply getting in a car and driving. Nowhere is ugly, no place is uninteresting in New Zealand, and you will never feel lost, lonely, or regret you came. I did not even mention what is perhaps the most famous walk in the world, the Milford Sound, only because I have not taken it. I must wait for our children to be a bit older. Fiordland is still unknown territory to us, but not for long. No country, I believe, rewards the inborn sense of adventure more than New Zealand, and if you were born without one, you will quickly acquire an urge to explore as soon as you set forth on your first road trip, whether by foot, bike, boat, or car, in this most extraordinary of countries.

Now you are on your own. Let me know what treasures you find: jeffreymasson@paradise.net.nz.

All the best,
Jeff

Should You Move to New Zealand?

*T*he short answer is "Yes." The longer answer is: "If you can get in." Things have tightened up here in the last few months, no doubt because so many people around the world suddenly, very suddenly, want to make a permanent move to New Zealand, post-9/11 and post–*Lord of the Rings*. It used to be considered the world's best-kept secret, but the secret is out and everybody knows a few important facts.

New Zealand is, at the moment I am writing, probably the safest place in the world to be. It also happens to be probably two of the most beautiful islands in the Pacific Ocean; it is not just green, but greener, maybe even greenest, in the most literal sense, cleaner than just about anywhere else simply because it is a tiny landmass surrounded by a vast ocean, so the pollution that settles down for a long stay in a place like, say, Mexico City, here just blows away with the first strong wind. People also know that it is, by first-world standards, still cheap. All of these secrets (known to only a few in the past) have now begun leaking so quickly that there has been a full-throttle rush to enter this paradise before the natives could assemble gates they could close against the well-heeled mobs clamoring for entrance.

It has not just been "foreigners" who wanted in. New Zealanders who had been living very well abroad were suddenly, after 9/11 (that is the magic date not just for America, but for many other places as well, and especially here), eager to return home. They felt their young children would be better off here than where they were, and they were mostly in the United States, England, and Australia. They had a point.

If you want your children to be outdoors a good part of the day, if it appeals to you that many in their classroom will go to school barefoot simply because they like to, then yes, New Zealand is the only place this is still possible. You could leave your eight-year-old in a playground and walk across the street to buy him some sushi (from a marvelous little hole in the wall called Cecil Takeaway on Tamaki Drive in St. Heliers, run by expert Korean cooks, our friends John and Vivian), as we did yesterday. Nobody would think twice about doing this here, but if you tried that in any large city in America, you could be charged with negligence. But you wouldn't because you would never dream of doing such a thing there (perhaps you could in certain countries of Europe—Denmark or Sweden, say). Now, I know that perception does not always equal reality, and we have seen that the statistics for child abuse, child poverty, and various other indicators in New Zealand show that not all is as it seems here. But perception does count, and it does mean something about what you will actually find in the real world: Your daily life in New Zealand with your kids is going to be far more pleasant than it would be just about anywhere else in the world. At least that is what I have experienced. Walking into town, playing on the beach, doing our shopping is easy, friendly, unthreatening. I have not once, in three years, felt nervous about walking anywhere near where I live, taking money out of a bank, hiking in almost vacant parks, walking on almost deserted beaches, driving on almost empty roads. This is not eerie here; this is normal. If you flag somebody down to ask for help, the person is likely not only to help you but also to then invite you to dinner in his or her modest but pristine farmhouse.

So you are not the only one who wants to come here. It has become much more difficult, since new immigration rules passed just a few months ago (perhaps in response to the escalating demand), especially if English is not your native tongue and you are not proficient. You really must know English well. If you are an older person, retired, then New Zealand will only welcome you if you invest at least half a million dollars (not in a house, though) in the country. But there is no reason not to do so if you have that kind of money, since there are many business opportunities in a country that is booming the way New Zealand currently is. If you are under fifty-six and professional, your chances of getting permanent residency are good, especially if you have worked for a while and have a job offer here. Doctors and engineers seem particularly welcome, although you will have to take qualifying exams. As of December 2003, there is also something called the Occupation Shortage List—that is, people with skills the government wants to encourage to immigrate—and if you qualify for this, then you do not even need a job offer. The list is long, among them: bakers, early childhood teachers, electrical engineers, graphic artists, anything in the field of biotechnology, IT specialists (with a bachelor of science degree and a major in computer science), anything to do with boats (for example, marine designer, marine engineer, yacht rigger), pharmacists, primary school teachers, veterinarians, and general practitioners. If you are a writer, you can apply for a business visa, and if you are a successful writer, you might well be qualified to remain in New Zealand on that ground alone. If you are thinking of starting a business here, and have a real plan, you are likely to get a three-year visa that can be fairly easily turned into a permanent one. In other words, if you have something to offer New Zealand, your chances of being able to stay here are still excellent. That did not apply to me, because I am too old (sixty-three); but I am lucky that my wife is both young (thirty-eight) and a doctor, so I got permanent residence because I belong to her family. The best place to check, however, is the website of New Zealand immigration: www.immigration.govt.nz. It might even be worth making the phone call from wherever you are: Dial 64 for New Zealand, 09 for Auckland, and then 9144100. Within minutes, remarkably, you will be talking to a real human being, and moreover, a friendly real human being!

(I just got off the phone with one, who was charming, helpful, and enthusiastic: "Do encourage your friends to move here," she told me with no irony intended.) They will send you tons of information and even on the phone you are likely to get a pretty good idea of your chances of moving here permanently, depending on your circumstances. The website also has a quick test you can take; by answering some simple questions you can determine whether it is worth your while to persist. I have a Swedish friend, Geeti Persson, who has been living in New Zealand for the last nine years as an immigration consultant. She is happy to advise you free of charge of your chances of immigrating here. Her email is: geeti@futurebusiness.co.nz and she has a website: wwww.futurebusiness.co.nz.

If you do get in, then of course your whole immediate family gets to come as well. This means that if you have older parents, they can come, too. That was the case with my mother, Diana Masson, who moved here last year when she was eighty-four. When we celebrated her eighty-fifth birthday a few weeks ago at her home across the street from the beach with her new friends, she said she had never been happier in her life, and only wished she had come here years ago. Once we have been permanent residents for three years (another year), she automatically gets permanent residence as well, which means she qualifies for free health care (right now we have private health insurance, which is remarkably cheap here, a few hundred dollars a year) and all the other benefits of an ordinary citizen. Speaking of which: I am also allowed to become a New Zealand citizen as soon as I have been a permanent resident for three years. But even before that, I have the right to vote, as soon as I am a permanent resident. And since America permits dual citizenship (were I to give up my American citizenship, it could be difficult to return, and after all, the Democrats cannot be out of power forever), I have just applied to become a New Zealand citizen!

Recommended Reading

History

Te Miringa Hohaia et al., editors. *Parihaka: The Art of Passive Resistance.* Wellington: Victoria University Press, 2001. The remarkable story of two charismatic Maori leaders, Te Whiti o Rongomai and Tohu Kakahi, who insisted on peaceful resistance to the invasion of their village in 1881. The Maori men of the village were taken prisoner for seventeen years!

Michael King. *Moriori: A People Rediscovered.* Auckland: Penguin, 1989 (rev. ed. 2000). Fascinating book by New Zealand's leading social historian about the people of Chatham Island (Rekohu) and their tragic attempts to live at peace with Maori invaders in the nineteenth century.

Gordon McLauchlan. *The Passionless People: New Zealanders in the 1970s.* Auckland: Cassell, 1976. A popular columnist dissects the Kiwi personality, not gently.

Literature

Alex Calder, editor. *The Writing of New Zealand: Inventions and Identities.* Auckland: Reed, 1993. Very useful collection of historical and literary pieces.

Travel

Robin Hanbury-Tenison. *Fragile Eden: A Ride Through New Zealand.* Topsfield, MA: Salem House, 1989. The president of Survival International and his wife ride horses through all New Zealand (as they had done earlier along the Great Wall of China), and give a sensitive portrayal of the land and the people.

J. B. Priestley. *A Visit to New Zealand.* London: Heinemann, 1974. "Before I set out I was in touch with an editor I knew, who declared firmly that he would welcome any contribution from me—*so long as it wasn't about New Zealand.*" One of the best books about New Zealand by an outsider that I have read.

NATURAL HISTORY

Gerard Hutching. *The Natural World of New Zealand: An Illustrated Encyclopaedia of New Zealand's Natural Heritage.* Auckland: Penguin, 1998. First place I went to find out about birds, trees, flowers, and anything to do with natural New Zealand.

R. M. Lockley. *Man Against Nature.* London: Andre Deutsch, 1970. Not to be missed, and readily available in secondhand-book stores in New Zealand. Lockley, who wrote *The Private Life of the Rabbit* (upon which *Watership Down* was based), came to live in New Zealand and was a great conservationist. But this book is more than a plea for conservation; it is a literate, impassioned account of the beauty of New Zealand.

Margaret Orbell. *The Natural World of the Maori.* Auckland: David Bateman, 1996 (rev. ed.). Only book of its kind.

Trevor H. Worthy and Richard N. Holdaway. *The Lost World of the Moa: Prehistoric Life of New Zealand.* Bloomington: Indiana University Press, 2002. The most complete and up-to-date account, technical but nonetheless fascinating.

TRAVEL GUIDE

I have found the best to be the Rough Guide. There is a new 2003 edition.

MAORI CULTURE

Cleve Barlow. *Tikanga Whakaaro: Key Concepts in Maori Culture.* Auckland: Oxford University Press, 1991.

J. Prytz Johansen. *Studies in Maori Rites and Myths.* Copenhagen: Ejnar Munksgaard, 1958.

Hirini Moko Mead. *Tikanga Maori: Living by Maori Values.* Wellington: Huia Publishers, 2003.

Margaret Orbell. *Waiata: Maori Songs in History: An Anthology Introduced and Translated by Margaret Orbell.* Auckland: Reed Books, 1991.

Margaret Orbell. *Traditional Maori Stories*. Bilingual Edition. Auckland: Reed Books, 1992.

Maggie Papakura (Makereti). *The Old-Time Maori*. Auckland: New Women's Press, 1986. First published in 1938 in London, this is the first ethnographic account of the Maori by a Maori ethnologist. Incomplete, but fascinating.

Glossary of New Zealand English Words and Expressions

Across the ditch—Australia.

Antipodes—A word commonly used in the Northern Hemisphere to refer to New Zealand/Australia—supposedly opposite Britain. **Antipodeans** live in both places.

Aotearoa—A modern (especially twenty-first-century) Maori name for New Zealand, meaning either "Land of the Long White Cloud" (which indeed you often see on the horizon); "Land of the Bright Waters"; or "Land of the Long Clear Day" (which it is!).

Are you there?—Used when answering the telephone instead of "Hello." (Advice: Do not respond, "No.")

Australasia—New Zealand, Australia, and their outlying islands.

Bach (pronounced "batch")—A small, simple house (suitable for a bachelor?) most often on the beach, and used primarily for weekends or holidays. Called a "crib" in the South Island.

Backblocks—Far off in the country. Other variants are **wop-wops** and also **up the booai** (from the little township of Puhoi, just north of Auckland).

Backpacker—A place where you rent an inexpensive room and share the kitchen, like a youth hostel.

Barbie—Barbecue.

Bittern—Known in Maori as the matuku, a rare (there are only a thousand left) New Zealand heron, with a song (considered deeply melancholy by the Maori) that carries for up to three miles.

Bloke—A guy.

Bludge—To borrow, by a **bludger** who is always borrowing.

Blue—A blunder, a mistake, an embarrassing error.

Bombay Hills—A place thirty miles south of Auckland, named for an immigrant ship, the *Bombay*, which arrived in 1865; most of the passengers settled in the gently rolling hills running east–west across this narrow portion of the North Island. **North of the Bombay Hills** is an expression (of contempt) for Auckland, whereas **south of the Bombay Hills** refers to the rest of New Zealand.

Bottler—Someone or something that is excellent, outstanding.

Brolly—Umbrella.

Bush—Forest, woods, usually reserved for native land. **To go bush** is just what it sounds like.

Bush lawyer—An amateur legal adviser. Also a thorny, climbing vine belonging to the blackberry family.

BYO—Bring your own beer or wine.

Cabbage tree—*Cordyline australis*, common throughout New Zealand; a tall, unusual tree (*not* a palm) used for food by the Maori and early settlers (some of whom said the soft young leaves from the center of the tree's head tasted like cabbage—hence the name—while others said they tasted like sweet, fresh almonds).

Capsicum—Sweet pepper.

Captain cooker—A wild pig.

Cheers—Good-bye; good luck.

Chemist—Pharmacy.

Chocker—Full.

Choice—Good, excellent, wonderful, as in the disdained (at least from a grammatical point of view) but common *cool as* and *good as* (with nothing following to make the comparison).

Chook—Chickens.

Chuffed—Excited, pleased, elated.

Cobber—Friend, buddy, mate.

Coconuts—Pacific Islanders. Offensive if used by others, but often used of themselves.

College—High school.

Corker—Wonderful, great; sometimes used ironically.

Crook—Feeling or looking ill, badly made, inedible. **To put you crook** is to mislead you.

Cuz—As in **Supcuz?** "What's up, friend?" Used by Pacific Islanders as **bro'**—both terms seem to have been borrowed from African American slang.

Cuzzy-bro—Term of address from one Maori to another.

Dag—An amusing character.

Dairy—A corner convenience store, almost uniquely owned by Indians from India or Fiji. Open all hours.

Dak—Marijuana; also magic **puha,** green tobacco.

Dinkum—True, fair, honest, genuine, first-rate.

Domain—Public park.

Down Under—Antipodean, hence Australia or New Zealand.

Eketahuna—A town in the Wairarapa District of the North Island whose odd-sounding Maori name intrigues New Zealanders, some of whom claim that nobody lives there, whereas, in fact, it is just an ordinary town.

Enzed—New Zealand.

Erewhon—*Nowhere* spelled backward; the name of a famous 1871 novel about utopia by the British writer Samuel Butler set in New Zealand in the Canterbury high country, where Butler owned five thousand acres and where he lived for four years before he returned to England and began his literary career.

Fair dinkum—True; or, Is it true?

Feijoa—An aromatic tropical green fruit, popular in California but almost unknown elsewhere in the United States—which is a pity since the juicy white pulp is tasty, low in calories, high in fiber, and a good source of vitamin C. The feijoa is originally from South America, but New Zealand has made a major effort to make the fruit popular.

Flatting—Sharing an apartment with somebody.

Fly cemetery—A small tart containing currants or raisins.

Fossick around—Explore.

Gallipoli—Name given by New Zealanders to Gelibolu in Turkey, the place where a major battle of World War I took place, with bad results for the Allied forces.

Get in behind—A sheep farmer's order for a dog to walk behind and wait for instructions.

Gidday—A common greeting in both New Zealand and Australia, as in **Gidday mate,** frequently heard. Also heard as **g'die.**

Godzone—God's own country, New Zealand.

Good as gold—All is well, right you are, agreed, fine, intact, fixed.

Grizzle—To complain.

Hard case—An eccentric, likable, funny, irrepressible individual. Used positively.

Hoon—A fool, a young lout.

Hori—Literally "George," a derisive term for Maori (included here for recognition purposes only; its use should be strictly avoided).

Jafa—A derisive term for a person from Auckland, literally "Just another fucking Aucklander." Commonly used in the South Island, tongue-in-cheek.

Joker—As in *ordinary Kiwi joker* or *real bloke*—the prototypical Kiwi male interested in beer, booze, and beach.

Jungle juice—Unsophisticated alcoholic beverage.

Katipo—The only poisonous spider in New Zealand, rarely, if ever, seen. Related to the U.S. black widow.

Kereru—A native wood pigeon—much larger, more colorful, and rarer than the city variety—who makes a loud swishing sound when it flies through the forest. Still seen, especially around the rain forest suburb of Titirangi in Auckland.

Kiwi—The now rare, flightless national bird, of which there were twelve million before human arrival in New Zealand; also the fruit (formerly called the Chinese gooseberry), and the people of New Zealand (along with their Kiwi accent).

Knackered—Exhausted. (Used almost exclusively by Kiwi men.)

Knock up—Assemble quickly.

Lifestyle block—A semirural property large enough for a home, garden, some animals, and perhaps a fruit orchard. The ideal retirement for many Kiwis. A hobby farm, looked down on by "real" farmers.

Lolly—Candy.

Long drop—An outdoor toilet (hole in the ground); also **dunny, dyke.**

Long paddock—Grass beside public roads, often the only grazing land for poor farmers to use, especially Maori farmers.

Mainland—The South Island. South Islanders speak of themselves as **mainlanders.**

Manuka—A native shrub, a tall tree-like bush, popular with bees, who produce very healthy manuka honey with antibiotic properties; also known as tea tree.

Mate—Close friend, or, used ironically, the opposite ("No way, mate").

Metal road—Unsealed, gravel, or dirt country road.

Mongrel Mob—A feared Maori gang, often in conflict with another gang, Black Power.

Morepork—A small, brown, native owl, *Ninox novaeseelandiae,* rarely seen but often heard and who seems to be saying these very words— "more pork"—in a slow, mournful way. Known as the ruru in Maori. Maori believe it is bad karma should they come indoors.

Mother country—England (obsolete).

Motor camp—A safe, clean place to stay with tent sites, cabins, and caravan (RV) sites.

Motorway—Freeway.

Muster—To round up sheep or cattle (hence **musterer**).

Nappy—Diaper.

Narked—Irritated, annoyed.

No worries—Easily accomplished, but lately used to mean "You're welcome."

Number 8 wire—A relatively thick wire used for fencing and for fixing, or making, just about anything else. Used of any ingenious repair, especially favored by rural Kiwis, who are very fond of **DIY** (do-it-yourself).

OE—Overseas experience—the time, usually in their twenties, when almost all New Zealanders spend at least a year abroad, in Australia, England, or the United States, in that order of preference.

Offside—In bad odor with. An **offsider,** on the other hand, is an assistant, especially of a cook, or a companion.

One out of the box—Used of anything especially fine.

Out of one's tree—Deranged, drunk, also tanked, sloshed, pissed, plastered, stonkered, cut, full as a tick, schickered. As in the United States and Australia, there are an endless and imaginative number of words to denote inebriation here.

Oz—Further abbreviation of "Aussie," or Australia.

Paddock—A word used for any field, no matter its size.

Pakeha—Pronounced with long vowels; a white New Zealander born in New Zealand of European or Caucasian descent; a non-Polynesian.

Panel beater—A body shop for cars, or a person who works at a body shop.

P.I.—Pacific Islander.

Piss—Beer.

Plunket Society—Free clinics for young babies throughout the whole of New Zealand. From the name of Lady Plunket, wife of an early governor of New Zealand (1904–10); formerly known as the Royal Society for the Protection of Women and Children.

Pohutukawa tree—*Metrosideros excelsa,* a huge, gnarled native tree with brilliant, bushy red flowers that bloom in December, especially common on sea cliffs in the north.

Pommy—Englishman, as in **whingeing Pommy,** an Englishman who complains about New Zealand.

Pongolia—Britain. (From **pongo,** British maritime slang for "marine.")

Poofter—An intellectually pretentious person.

Possie—Position.

Pukeko—*Porphyrio porphyrio melanotus,* a swamp-loving native bird, resembling a black-purple-red hen. Very adaptable and cheeky.

Puriri—A tall (up to seventy-five feet), thick (up to eight feet in girth), handsome, native pink-blossomed, red-fruited tree (*Vitex lucens*), often with epiphytes in its thick branches, much loved by native birds such as the kereru, tui, and bellbird for food; by Maori for ulcers and sore throats; and by me, for the way it looks.

Rellies—Relatives, and also **pressie** (present), **veggies** (vegetables), the **postie** (postman, who delivers the mail on his **walkies**), the **chippie** (carpenter), **woody** (a woodsman), **wharfies** (longshoremen), a **sammie** (sandwich), the **sparky** (electrician), and the several **cockies** (farmers), notably the **sheep-cocky** (sheep farmer) and **cow-cocky** (dairy farmer).

Rifleman—The smallest bird in New Zealand.

Rock College—Mount Eden Prison in Auckland.

Root—To rape.

Scoria—Porous, lightweight dark rock—lava fragments—widely used in building and for roads, especially in Auckland.

Scrubber—Small child.

Section—A large plot of land.

Sheila—A slightly derogatory (in my opinion) generic term for "woman," comparable to *the wife.* Used of a youngish, desirable woman.

She'll be right—Everything will turn out fine, even if it appears unlikely, so stop worrying, it's unnecessary.

Shout—To pick up the tab, as in **to shout a drink.**

Skite—To brag, especially about oneself. Bad form here.

Skive—To leave in the lurch.

Sleep-out—A small backyard shed.

Spit the dummy—To have a temper tantrum.

Spuds—Potatoes.

State house—An inexpensive rental home built by the former Labour government, often sold now for much higher prices.

Station—A large farm.

Stonkered—Beaten.

Strine—Australian (especially the language).

Sweet—Cool, okay, perfect.

Ta—Thanks.

Tall poppy—High-profile in a negative sense: standing out, too conspicuous, in need of being cut down to size. Central to New Zealand self-image. The **great Kiwi clobbering machine** takes care of him or her.

Tamarillo—Popular, delicious tropical fruit, also known as tree tomato.

Tane Mahuta—God of the forest, an enormous kauri tree in Waipoua Kauri Forest, estimated to be twelve hundred years old and sacred to the Maori. Worth the trip (north of Auckland).

Taniwha—A water dragon in Maori mythology (pronounced "Tanifa").

Terminal lift—Rising intonation, making every statement sound like a question, especially used among young people, not just here, but in America as well; a form of Valley-talk: "Hi, my name is Kristy? I'm here to serve you?" Not a question.

The dees—Detectives.

The Other Side—Australia.

Tinny—Exceptionally lucky, unexpectedly lucky; also, a small quantity of marijuana.

Togs—Bathing suit.

Totara—A tall type of pine tree much admired for its strength by the Maoris, hence the term *the mighty totara fell*.

Tramping—Hiking.

Trundler—Shopping cart.

Tuatara—A long-living (up to a hundred years!) reptile, with a mysterious third eye, that resembles a lizard but isn't one. The species dates back 220 million years, to the age of dinosaurs; all of its relatives are now fossils. Fewer than a hundred thousand survive.

Tucker—Food. **Dog tucker** means past history, written off, finished.

He's dog tucker: He's doomed. **Tuckered out** means extremely tired, exhausted.

Tui—A native nectar-eating bird (*Prosthemadera novaeseelandiae*) with an amazing repertoire and range of songs, sounds, and ability to mimic (cats, people, or more frequently other birds) as well as a strong sense of family (generations live close to one another). Also known as the parson bird because of a tuft of white feathers around the neck.

Tussock—Native grasses of various species, which grow in clumps on hills and mountains.

Varsity—University.

Village—Main shopping street (local center) of a small town or suburb.

Waikikamukau—Imaginary rural town name; backblocks. Maori–Pakeha hybrid nonsense name: "Why kick a moo cow."

Weetabix—Breakfast cereal—used derogatorily for compressed-particleboard construction material.

Weta—From *wetapunga*, the giant weta, who lives primarily in treetops, this is a local insect similar to a grasshopper and cricket, of ferocious mien but quite harmless, unchanged for the last 190 million years. One of the hundred species of weta is known as a cave weta, *Pharmacus montanus,* and can jump up to ten feet! Several species, including the tusked weta, were only discovered in the last few years.

Whinge—To complain, to whine, as in **whingeing pommy,** an Englishman who is not happy with the way things are in New Zealand.

Winterless north—Name used for the North Auckland peninsula seen as a near-tropical paradise. Exaggerated, but not entirely inaccurate. "The North," so sparsely populated, is considered a law unto itself.

Wowser—A puritanical spoilsport.

Glossary of Maori Words

Following is a brief list of Maori words I found commonly used in books about New Zealand; it is meant only as a helpful guide to reading, not as a means of learning the beautiful Maori language, something I heartily recommend to anyone who plans to live here. New Zealand is meant to be, and should be, a bilingual country, like Canada. I have taken the words from various sources: friends, neighbors, history books like *The Oxford History of New Zealand*, literary works such as Keri Hulme's novel *The Bone People*, as well as many glossaries, dictionaries, and vocabularies I have consulted. Often Maori words in novels and nonfiction books go untranslated, so this glossary might prove helpful.

Ae—Yes.

Anana!—Behold! There you are! An exclamation of surprise.

Ariki—The highest-ranking male or female of a chiefly family.

Aroha—Love, friendship, compassion, sympathy.

Atua—Spirit, god.

Awa—River.

E hoa—Friend; also, an exclamation of surprise or disgust.

E koro—Elder (as term of address). **E kui** refers to an elderly woman. **E pou** is an affectionate term of respect for any old person.

E tama!—Man!

Haere mai—Welcome (literal meaning: "Come to me"). Often seen on signs coming into a town.

Haere ra—Farewell.

Haka—A passionate dance, often translated as "war dance," where ferocious sounds and gestures are loudly declaimed. There are also welcoming hakas, good-bye hakas, and many other forms. See the one performed at the main museum in Auckland.

Hakari—Feast, gift, symbolic meal.

Hangi—An earth oven and the ceremony around the food prepared this way, similar to a Hawaiian luau.

Hapu—Subtribe or clan; also, extended family; also, to be pregnant.

Hau—Wind.

Hawaiki—The never completely identified place from which the Maori came to New Zealand, hence the homeland.

Hikoi—A protest march.

Hoha—Fuss, nuisance, angry, frustrated, fed up, bored.

Hokioi—A legendary bird.

Hongi—A traditional greeting, where noses are pressed (and held for a few moments) but lips do not touch.

Huhu—A large beetle, also Maori warrior.

Hui—A formal meeting, or assembly, where rituals are observed; mainly for Maori only.

Ihi—Power, authority, essential force.

Ika—Fish.

Inanga—Whitebait, *Galaxias maculatus*.

Iwi—Tribe, kin.

Kai—Food, as in **kaimoana,** seafood; also, a prefix referring to somebody who does something.

Kainga—A village, usually of a single tribe. Home.

Kai-tiaki—Guardian.

Kakariki—Parakeet; also, the color green, and green gecko.

Ka kite ano—See you, good-bye.

Kanga—Curse.

Kapai—Great, good.

Karakia—A formal address to a higher power, similar to prayer, incantation.

Karanga—To call; ceremonial call; a haunting, melodious chant sung usually by one woman, to initiate a ceremony.

Kaumatua—A Maori elder of either sex, a cross between a sage and a therapist; also, head of the family, and a word for "adult."

Kaupapa—Plan, ideas, philosophy, as in **kura kaupapa Maori,** a primary school with teaching methods based on Maori language and culture.

Kawa—Etiquette observed on a marae.

Kawanatanga—Governance.

Kehua—Ghost.

Kei te pai—All right, that's right.

Kete—Basket

Kia ora—(pronounced as one word, more like "kyora") A common way of beginning anything, slightly more complex than *hello* and not nearly as corny as *aloha* in Hawaii. Although Pakeha may find it affected, Maori definitely like it when you use this greeting. Slightly more formal is **tena koe** (to one person) or **tena koutou katoa** (to several people). Also thank you, hello, to your health (when drinking).

Kikorangi—Deep blue, sky blue.

Kingitanga—Maori King Movement.

Kiore—A native rat, brought to the islands by the Maori for food.

Koha—Gift, donation.

Kohanga reo—Literally "language nest," a preschool taught entirely in Maori (but non-Maori are welcome). These started only in 1981 and are increasingly popular.

Kohuru—To kill by stealth, to deal treacherously.

Korero—Speech, talk.

Koro—Old man, grandfather.

Koru—The uncurling young fern, much loved by Maori as a symbol of renewal.

Kotahitanga—Maori unity.

Kouka—Cabbage tree.

Koura—Crayfish.

Kuia—A wise older woman, the female equivalent of *kaumatua*; also, grandmother.

Kukupa—Native pigeon.

Kumara—A sweet potato, brought by the first canoes to New Zealand, and very important to subsistence there. Considered almost a sacred food.

Kupapa—Neutral, but used for Maori who fought on the government's side in various anti-Maori wars.

Makomako—Bellbird.

Makutu—Sorcery, witchcraft.

Mana—Prestige, dignity, power, influence. Used of people and of places. Never self-bestowed (boasting is tapu in Maori society). **Manawhenua** is the right of an iwi, hapu, or whanau to claim land through genealogy, occupation and use, or conquest.

Manaki—Compassion.

Mangai—Mouth.

Mango—Shark.

Manu—Bird. Also the name of our son! **Manumea** is a sacred bird.

Manuhiri—Guest, visitor.

Maori—The people living in New Zealand for the last eight hundred years. Literally, the term means something like "natural" or "normal." A fairly recent term, it is in general use. Pronounced with a long *a* and long *o*, simply by lingering over these two vowels. Not "Mori."

Marae—A meeting place with a building and dramatic carvings. Every Maori place has one.

Matamua—Firstborn son.

Mate—Dead. **Mate Maori** is Maori sickness, caused by a curse, witch-craft, or breach of tapu.

Matemateone—Love for all creation.

Matua—A parent of either sex, but especially a father.

Maunga—A hill, or a mountain. Commonly found with place-names.

Mauri—Life principle, essence (pronounced "mori").

Mere—A hand weapon made of greenstone or bone.

Mihi—Greeting ceremony. **Mihimihi** are formal speeches during the mihi.

Mimi—Urine.

Moa—Originally the Polynesian word for "domestic chicken," it was used for the giant (taller than a man) flightless vegetarian bird of the order Dinornithiformes in existence for fifteen million years, but hunted to extermination by about 1500 largely because they were defenseless and inoffensive birds who had no reason to believe any-body meant them any harm.

Moana—Ocean.

Moana-nui-a-Kiwa—Pacific Ocean.

Moko—Maori tattoo (also the word for "lizard"). Those elaborate designs on the face, legs, and arms were traditionally burned into the skin. Recently very fashionable, but originally a visual sign of descent, rank, and family.

Mokopuna—Grandchild.

Motu—Island, often used in combination with other words, as a place-name.

Muru—To take compensation from an offender.

Na!—Drawing attention to something. There! That is it!

Nau mai—Welcome.

Nei (or *ne*)?—Meaning "Right?," "Isn't that so?" The term functions much like the French *n'est-ce pas?*

Nga—Plural of "the."

Ngati—The first word of various tribe names.

Noa—Free from tapu.

Ora—Alive, well, well-being.

Oriori—A sleep-time chant, lullaby.

Pa—A Maori fortification, or village.

   E Pa!—Dad!

Pakaru—Broken.

Pakeha—Non-Maori.

Papa—Earth.

Papa-tu-nuk—Earth Mother.

Patu—Beat, treat badly, kill.

Pipi—An edible smooth-shelled shellfish.

Pipi (with long i's)—Young.

Piripiri—A term of endearment for children.

Po—Night.

   Hine-nui-te-Po—Goddess of death.

Poi—A light ball, attached to a string, used in singing and dancing.

Ponga—The silver tree fern; also, the building material of a fence or house.

Porangi—Crazy, mad, insane, deranged.

Potiki—Youngest child.

Pounamu—Greenstone, also known as New Zealand jade (though it isn't; it's a form of nephrite), highly prized by the Maori for making brightly polished ornaments in different shades of green, and weapons.

Powhiri—(pronounced "pofiri") A formal Maori welcome.

Puha—A soft, green, edible thistle. Also called sowthistle. **Electric puha** is locally grown marijuana.

Puku—Tummy.

Puna—Spring of water.

Pupu—An edible green snail, also called a cat's eye.

Rahui—A ban on the taking of birds, fish, and other animals. Clearly, the Maori were aware of the ecological effects of overhunting.

Raiona—Transliteration of "lion."

Rangatira—Chief; aristocrat.

Rangi—The sky (sky-father).

Rangi-nui-a-Tane—Sky Father.

Raupo—Bulrush.

Rohe—A territorial area claimed by an iwi, hapu, or whanau, including all resource rights.

Rongoa—Medicine, remedy.

Runanga—Assembly, council.

Taha Maori—A Maori perspective, or Maori way of doing something.

Taiaha—A carved longstaff.

Taihoa—Slow down, wait, delay, deliberate policy of procrastination.

Tamaiti—Child.

Tamariki—Children.

Tane—Man.

Tane Mahuta—God of the forest.

Tangaroa—God of the sea.

Tangata—Human beings, people.

Tangata kino—Bad person.

Tangata whenua—People of the land—the Maori name for Maori people.

Tangi—Death ceremonial, or lament. **Tangihanga** is a funeral wake, but a longer, more elaborate affair, often lasting days, weeks, or even months.

Taonga—Treasure, physical or intangible; the Maori language is a taonga.

Tapu—Taboo, forbidden because of a sacred connection (such as land that cannot be entered).

Taua muru—A group of people engaged in plundering.

Taumau (also **Tomo**)—An arranged marriage.

Taurekareka—A slave. This was not a hereditary status: The children of slaves were by custom born free.

Tawhirimatea—God of the Winds.

Te—The.

Te Ao—The world of light.

Teina—Younger sibling, or cousin of the same sex.

Tena koutou—Greetings to you (plural).

Te Po—Primeval darkness before creation.

Te reo—The Maori language.

Tika—Right, just, fair, correct, done according to traditional ways.

Tikanga—Traditional practices, as in **tikanga Maori,** referring to Maori values, the Maori way of doing things.

Tiki—A pendant, often made of greenstone, worn as jewelry, of a peculiar figure looking like a fetus in sleep.

Tino kino—Very bad.

Titi—The muttonbird (so called because the nestlings are killed for oil, feathers, and meat—products similar to those from sheep), really a sooty shearwater, a seabird. When the word is pronounced with two short i's, it means to stab, or steep.

Toetoe—A kind of grasslike sedge.

Toheroa—A large edible marine bivalve shellfish commonly used for soup.

Tohunga—A traditional medicine man, priestly expert; also, a specialist, as in **tohunga whakairo,** a carving specialist.

Tuahu—A sacred place where rituals are performed.

Tuakana—Elder brother, sister, or cousin.

Tuna—Eel.

Tupuna (also *tipuna*)—A grandparent of either sex, along with all the relatives of the same generation; an ancestor.

Turangawaewae—Home, place to stand, birthplace, identity based on homeland, the place where one stands firm and secure.

Tutu—A tree with poisonous seeds; if the second u is pronounced long, it means to fiddle about, to tamper with, to adjust. **To eat one's toot** is to adapt to country ways.

Tupakihi—Native shrub (highly poisonous) whose leaves or pulp had medicinal use for broken limbs.

Tutua—Commoner.

Tuturu—In the phrase *he Maori tuturu:* a person descended from Maori only, or a person steeped in Maori culture.

Urupa—Burial ground.

Utu—Vengeance, but of wider significance: payback, return action, satisfaction, compensation, reciprocity. Used in both the negative and positive senses (the latter as in hospitality rendered, or an act done to restore some sort of balance).

Wahi—Place.

Wahine—Woman. Pronounced with a long *a*, the word means women.

Wai—Water.

Waiata—A song.

Wairua—Essence, the spirit of something, image, shadow.

Waitapu—Sacred water.

Waka—A wooden, dug-out canoe, including the very ones the Maori used to come to Aotearoa from Hawaiki. Also used for the group of tribes based on common descent from these migratory canoeists.

Wananga—Learning, specialized knowledge of the tohunga.

Wero—A challenge (either to start a fight or to avoid one).

Whakama—Shame.

Whakapapa (pronounced "fakapapa")—Genealogy, ancestral history, relationship; also, the study of genealogies.

Whanau—Immediate and extended family.

Whare—House.

Wharenui—Meetinghouse.

Whare puni—Sleeping quarters.

Whare wananga—University.

Whenua—Land, ground, placenta.

Wiwi—Rushes. The word also refers to the French.